Emotions @ Work

Get Better Results by Encouraging Accountability and Resolving Conflicts

By

Faith A. Ralston, Ph.D.

ISBN: 0-7596-7422-1 (e-book)
ISBN: 0-7596-7423-X (Paperback)
ISBN: 0-7596-7424-8 (Dustjacket)

This book is printed on acid free paper.

1stBooks - rev. 06/21/02

Dedication

This book is dedicated to my father, who was a minister,
and to my dad, who was a man;
and to my mother, whose playful spirit
lives in my soul.

Acknowledgments

I am grateful to the following individuals for their trust, encouragement and enthusiasm as I wrote this book:

My children, David, Andrew, Stuart and Peter Ralston, who encouraged me and brought me back to normal life as I worked night and day on this book.

Ruth and Bill Bostock, my aunt and uncle, who have loved me unconditionally since the moment I was born.

Jill Konrath, my friend and colleague, who walks with me on my life's journey.

John Macdonald, a friend and mentor, who is always there for me at precisely the right moment.

Joanne, Chuck and Bass Bay Resort, who in their nurturing, plus quiet and consistent encouragement, supported me as I wrote.

Davis Balestracci, for his avid support and use of these ideas in the classroom to help employees harness emotions and improve their work situations.

Special thanks to Bert Hellinger for his powerful work in Family Constellations, which connected me to my lineage; Jamie Champion of HoloChromataic Life Sciences, whose transforming perspectives helped me appreciate my unique talents; and Elleva Joy McDonald, whose dynamic movement classes and healing insights enabled me to become who I am.

Preface

The heart has its reason which reason does not understand.

Blaise Pascal

Why This Book?

In my role as a business consultant and psychologist, I am privy to feelings and concerns that are not openly expressed in the work setting. Managers and employees share their fears about pending changes, mistrust of peers, concern about job security and conflict with bosses and employees.

After twelve years of working in the areas of quality and organizational change, I became discouraged. I saw managers undermine each other's efforts, employees suppress their opinions and worthwhile projects fail as hidden agendas and ego needs sabotaged their success. From this place of frustration, the ideas and concepts in this book were born.

My purpose in writing this book is to get to the heart of the problems we all experience some time at work. I address the unspoken dynamics that keep us silent when we need to talk, "closed" when we need to cooperate and fearful when we need to trust. You will learn how honest feelings and opinions are an untapped resource that can contribute to your business success.

Specifically, you will discover the unwritten contract that governs employment relationships, the impact of fear on business decisions and how hidden agendas work against ideal solutions. The eight principles of emotions will help you address specific work issues such as career dilemmas, negative work environments, problems with employees and succeeding with change. The "new" role of the manager is defined and action steps are provided to help you resolve conflicts, develop trust and facilitate better communication.

This is not a sit-on-the-shelf book but rather one that is meant to be used. Each chapter includes important ideas, principles, case examples and ways to encourage implementation. My hope is that you will enhance your ability to welcome the expression of honest feelings, recognize and reward individual worth and see their direct link to business performance. The benefit of these ideas-in-action is people who fully contribute their talents and organizations that prosper.

Contents

Ten Business Realities and Success Actions

Business Reality #1: We can no longer succeed in business without taking down the walls between us.
Success Action: Stop corporate craziness to get better results.

Business Reality #2: Emotions impact how we feel, what we do and whether we're successful at work.
Success Action: Harness emotional energy to improve business performance.

Business Reality #3: What bothers us the most are the things we don't talk about.
Success Action: Learn facts about feelings to positively affect the bottom line.

Business Reality #4: Conflicts and resentments thwart good business performance.
Success Action: Defuse hot buttons to reduce conflicts at work.

Business Reality #5: Up to fifty percent of time in an organization is wasted due to mistrust.
Success Action: Address hidden dynamics to improve business decisions.

Business Reality #6: Seventy percent of employees are afraid to speak up for fear of negative repercussions.
Success Action: Drive out fear to promote exceptional communication.

Business Reality #7: Current work requires radically different behaviors than imprints from the past.
Success Action: Adopt new leadership roles to meet changing work requirements.

Business Reality #8: The majority of employees who quit their job are actually quitting their manager.
Success Action: Develop mutual respect to strengthen supervisory relationships.

Business Reality #9: We contribute more when we love what we're doing.
Success Action: Leverage individual talents to deliver higher value.

Business Reality #10: Bottled-up concerns drain vital energy away from key initiatives.
Success Action: Initiate candid conversations to implement change faster.

Chapter 1

Stop Corporate Craziness To Get Better Results

We are citizens of the world; and the tragedy of our times is that we do not know this.

Woodrow Wilson

Cara: What a *day* I'm having!
Luke: What's going on?
Cara: It's my boss. He's sending Jordan to the marketing meeting in Atlanta instead of me.
Luke: What! How can he do that? You've been planning to go for over a year.
Cara: I know! He decided to let Jordan give the presentation—not *me.*
Luke: Have you talked to him about it?
Cara: Are you kidding? He's a *jerk.*

Conflicts like this happen every day at work—and they affect us deeply. With friends, spouses or colleagues, we talk about work a lot. We talk about whom we like, what we think, the situations we encounter and frustrations we feel. Yet on the job only a trusted few know what we really think.

Conflicts thwart our success. It's estimated that up to fifty percent of time in organizations is wasted because of trust issues. Business challenges such as e-commerce, a global economy and competitive pressures demand levels of collaboration and teamwork we never dreamed possible. The time is past when we can pursue independent agendas, permit internal groups to be at war and allow politics to get in the way of established priorities. Business success depends on our ability to trust each other, share resources and build bridges across physical and psychological distances.

Organizational Craziness

The new ways of working are a lot more chaotic and unorganized than we'd like them to be. We're moving away from hierarchical structures to flatter, leaner, more fluid organizations. We do so because we possess neither the human nor the financial resources to survive any other way.

Today the boss is never there, department lines are unclear and we move in and out of projects quickly. Major initiatives are accomplished with scant resources, tight timelines and marginal budgets. We worry about what's going to happen if the new product fails, our funding gets cut or a merger puts us out of business. We're anxious about losing our jobs, customers, opportunities and resources.

Organizational craziness is "terror in action." It's manic, anxious behavior caused by our fears. When one person catches it, especially at the top, it spreads like wildfire. Just beneath the surface lurk fear and uncertainty about the changes that assail us. Rather than calm ourselves, we reflect each other's anxieties and keep the frenzy alive.

We work twenty-four hours a day, seven days a week—via e-mail, faxes and cell phones—to meet deadlines and complete projects. Mary, an executive manager in a utility company, reflects on her experience after leaving a high-level job: "I can hardly believe how caught up I got in the craziness. I worked 70 to 85 hour work weeks and when I look back at the projects, they seem meaningless! How could I get so wrapped up? Now, it seems like another world; I just scratch my head. But when I was there, everything seemed critical!"

We're continually stressed and anxious. Don, a venture manager, confessed, "Every night I go home scared to death. I don't know if this new venture is going to make it. I'm afraid to tell my people. Around them I demonstrate confidence and a sense of assurance, but I don't feel that way inside." Without our connection to each other it's easy to feel alone.

Symptoms

Symptoms of corporate craziness abound. We're not able to focus on one thing long enough to get it done. We go from meeting to meeting—scattered, barely attentive, leaving loose ends and confusion in our wake. There's never enough time. Weeks go by in a blur of activity. We can't distinguish one day from the next. Everything is urgent. The pressure never subsides. There's always a crisis that needs our attention. We're tightly wound, unable to settle down and consider the implications and consequences of our actions.

There's No Time!

We pride ourselves on the number of balls we can keep in the air. A group of exhausted employees asks an executive to prioritize 150 initiatives. He refuses, saying: "Everything is important! If I prioritize one, the others won't get done." We're overwhelmed by the amount of work there is to do, and we rarely feel the satisfaction of seeing a project well done. To keep things going we delegate to others, but we don't have time to explain what we need. We don't have time for our personal lives. Spouses, families and friends are seen as intrusions on our busy schedules. Our attention is on deadlines, which are poor indicators of important priorities.

Manic Use of Technology

Technology further enables us to act out the craziness. Mary, a sales manager, describes talking to a peer, Al, on his car phone. During their conversation Al puts her on hold four times to answer incoming calls. Finally he asks Mary to call him back because he's receiving a fax in his car. In Al's world there's little time to plan, learn or reflect.

Too Busy to Care

Our offices are filled with people working under the same roof for the same organization who don't know each other's name. Once I was looking for a faculty member, Jim, at a large university. I couldn't find him so I asked a woman on his floor if she knew where he was located. "No," she responded, "I don't know a Jim; perhaps he's on a different floor." I started to take the elevator when I noticed a sign for Jim's office right next to *her* office. Jim worked less than twenty feet away, yet she didn't know he existed. This is corporate craziness. We don't have time to care.

Organizational Depression

We can exist in this frenetic state of activity for only so long. After a while we become adversely affected. Layoffs, restructuring, new business strategies and changing job requirements leave us numb, depressed and silently discontent. We feel whipsawed and no longer want to play. Vitality is missing. One research report states that eighty percent of employees feel their jobs are "meaningless." New programs don't excite us and motivational speeches can't overcome our skepticism. We feel, "What's the use? Nothing's going to change. Why bother?" We bite our tongues—even though a small voice inside of us says, "This is nuts!" We lose our confidence, overwork to prove ourselves, then doubt the value of our contributions.

We become used to the craziness. It's what everyone else is doing. We don't believe it can be any different. Obeying the rules and fitting in is the barter we make for job security and our good standing with others. It's easier to catch the craziness than to find a new way to work together.

Action Exercise

1. Check how many symptoms of corporate craziness you observe in your workplace.

    _____ Lack of focus or direction
    _____ Frenetic behaviors
    _____ Obsession with technology
    _____ Attitude of being too busy
    _____ Depression/don't care
    _____ Crisis orientation
    _____ Judgmental attitudes
    _____ Tendency to be secretive about decisions
    _____ Indirect or vague communication
    _____ Intolerance for mistakes
    _____ Excessive closed-door conversations
    _____ Reactive budgeting processes
    _____ Too many unproductive meetings

2. Identify the ways you participate in the craziness:

    - What I do that doesn't make sense is: _______________
    - If I were brave, I would stop doing: _________________
    - I question the effectiveness of the following activities:
      ____

3. Choose actions you can take to stop corporate craziness in your work life:

    - I could stop doing: _______________________________
    - I can better understand why we do: _________________
    - I could improve the way we do: _____________________

Inability to Work Together

Corporate craziness is caused by our inability to work together. We compete to get ahead, protect our budgets and fill our department with the maximum head count we can justify. However, these behaviors no longer suit us or our organizations. Denise, a human resource manager from a national retail company, says it well: "We've mastered all the technical aspects of business, but the real challenges are the human ones—despite our success, people are still unable to reach agreement or work collaboratively and share resources. We can't get people to trust each other."

Our typical ways of relating are as outdated and ineffective as the technologies of yesterday. They still work, as do the typewriters of old, but they are no longer adequate to respond to the challenges we face. The inability to work together is costing us far more than any external threat. To succeed we must make the quality of our business relationships as important as our strategies, budgets and schedules.

The new bottom line in business is that we need each other. Complex solutions and fast time-to-market can be achieved only by clarity of vision and effective collaboration. We need agreement on outcomes, innovative solutions and successful implementation. No one person, group or authority has all the answers. Intelligent decisions require input from many sources, calm discussion of implications, appropriate time to plan, and trust that allows us to implement these decisions.

Finding a Way Out of the Craziness

It takes courage to do things differently. To change the game we must take down the walls between us. The benefits are significant. We will have:

- Less stress
- Higher motivation

- Improved job performance
- Greater honesty and candor
- Better understanding of the real issues

To achieve this we need to create communities where we can bring more of who we are to work. We must foster the courage and provide a safe atmosphere for people to share their personal experiences. We must create healthful work environments where employees can confront bosses; where business decisions are challenged; where it's safe to say, "I'm not happy here"; where rocking the boat is expected, honesty is the norm and deep feelings are shared. Honest opinions and feelings are the untapped resources that will help us and our organizations prosper.

We start by having candid conversations with coworkers and bosses and asking fundamental questions such as these:

- How well are we getting along?
- Are we communicating effectively?
- Do we know what to expect from each other?
- Do we trust each other?
- Are we comfortable working together?
- What specifically can we improve?

The answers to these questions are powerful indicators of our ability to get work done.

Workplace as Community

I like to compare the norms and behaviors of our current organizational life with the pioneer communities of the nineteenth century. In this culture work meant the difference between starving and having shelter and enough food to eat. These pioneers knew how to cooperate. They held profoundly different feelings and attitudes about relationships at work.

Barn-raising is a wonderful symbol of that time when family, friends and neighbors came together to support a newlywed couple or family in need. Everyone pitched in, contributed food and shared the work until the job was done. People participated in each other's lives and everyone was involved. Sometimes they gave help, other times they received it, and somehow it all worked out. The people they worked with were also the people they played with and prayed with.

In order to create a sense of community, we must be able to take to work more of who we are, how we feel and what is happening to us. We are not meant to be isolated islands in the sea, impervious to the icy water around us. We're more like the soft-shell clam, protected by its shell. However, in order to eat and be nourished, the clam must open up its shell and be vulnerable. For us to be nourished at work, we must shuck our psychological armor and start sharing our needs, feelings, concerns and vulnerabilities. It's imperative that we build a new kind of workplace—a workplace that supports us as we take greater personal responsibility for our work and our personal lives.

A Hopeful Vision

In place of corporate craziness we can transform our workplaces into communities that support personal and professional change, respect individual differences, respond to customers and possess an unwavering commitment to quality products and services. The purpose of this new work community is twofold:

1. To respond to the needs of the world and its customers in a brilliant and creative way.

2. To foster and support the personal and professional growth of the individuals who serve in it.

As managers and employees inside these communities, we welcome the opportunity to look beyond our functional areas and consider what's good for the whole. We realize that we can't do it alone. We must become experts at building relationships, identifying and alleviating concerns and resolving our differences. We can find our way out of the craziness by discovering the quiet center of our connection with each other.

Business Reality #1: We can no longer succeed in business without taking down the walls between us.

Success Action: Stop corporate craziness to get better results.

Key Learnings:

1. The new bottom line in business is that we need each other.

2. Our usual ways of relating to each other are as outdated as the technologies of yesterday.

3. Corporate craziness is symptomatic of our inability to work together.

4. The quality of our relationships with coworkers is as relevant to business success as are our strategies, budgets and schedules.

5. Honest opinions and authentic feelings are the untapped resources that will help us and our organizations prosper.

Chapter 2

Harness Emotional Energy To Improve Business Performance

He is a fine friend. He stabs you in the front.

Leonard Lewis Levinson

Are you stewing and unhappy about something at work? Every day you and the people you work with make decisions about what you're going to address and what you're going to ignore. The net result of these decisions is nothing less than your ability to achieve business success.

Assessment

Answer the following questions to identify how fully you can share your feelings and opinions at work:

1. Do you have ideas that you haven't shared about areas at work that could be improved?

   Yes *No*

2. Are there issues that your group isn't discussing that need to be addressed?

   Yes *No*

3. Are you worried about someone's reaction to a change but haven't asked him or her about it?

   Yes *No*

4. Are you silently questioning a decision that makes no sense to you?

Yes *No*

5. Are you avoiding interaction with someone you need to collaborate with?

Yes *No*

6. Are you frustrated daily by a colleague's actions but hesitate to say anything?

Yes *No*

Projects at work stall when we waste precious time and energy on conflicts and trust issues. Then decisions get made for the wrong reasons, deadlines aren't met and we end up running in place rather than reaching our goals. Conversely, when we trust each other, feel free to share our opinions and successfully address the issues, we make gigantic leaps forward.

Despite the business impact of good working relationships, it's a hit-or-miss proposition whether we're successful in this area. Even strong leaders fold when confronted with interdepartmental wars, conflicts and performance issues. We can no longer leave this area of good working relationships to chance or chemistry. We need to learn how to work together. Specifically, we must be able to:

- Create environments where people feel safe to share their thoughts, feelings and insights in a constructive way.
- Foster feelings of hope and enthusiasm for change and calm feelings of anxiety and worry about the future.
- Take responsibility for creating good working relationships, despite past resentments and personality clashes.
- Respond wisely to emotional reactions and move past conflicts toward effective solutions.

- Motivate ourselves and others to take consistent action toward our goals, despite immediate setbacks and disappointments.

We must learn how to harness the incredible power of emotions to meet our business challenges. Never has the need for this been so great. Turbulent work environments activate intense emotions in even the most composed individual. Emotional energy is powerful and vital. Like a wild horse full of potential, our emotional energy can be harnessed and tamed to help us achieve extraordinary results. Positive emotional energy creates compelling visions, ignites enthusiasm for new initiatives and helps us work collaboratively. We need this powerful force and we fear its power.

Emotions Forced Underground

Organizational life requires that we work side-by-side, eight to twelve hours a day, five days a week. We spend more time with coworkers than we do with our friends, significant others or children. Our feelings and opinions don't go away just because we go to work. In the morning we can put on our work clothes, but we cannot take off our emotions.

Each of us experiences every feeling possible: anger, joy, jealousy, love, sadness, hope, guilt and fear (see Figure 2-1). In the workplace, our emotional needs manifest as resentments, conflicts, retiring on-the-job, petty turf wars, emotional outbursts and sabotage. It's unrealistic to think we can completely set aside our emotions at work.

Figure 2-1: Universal feelings

So what happens to our emotions when we go to work? They go underground and become a powerful invisible force. Hours, days, months, sometimes years are spent protecting ourselves from people we don't trust, avoiding problems we can't talk about, working around performance issues, feigning acceptance to decisions and putting up with jobs that aren't right for us. Our honest feelings are hidden, denied and choked back, but rarely used to help solve our problems.

When I interview employees about issues at work, a flood of opinions, insights and feelings come pouring out. Often it's as if a dam has burst. These same employees say, "Don't tell anyone I said this!" The things that bother us the most are the things we won't talk about.

We Have Inner Gyroscopes

When unpleasant emotions are present, we know it. We feel them, regardless of whether they are shared openly. We have an "inner gyroscope" that tells us when things aren't right. It's a survival instinct. At work we know when our star is rising, whether a peer disapproves of us and if we're in sync with what's going on. We can sense layoffs coming. We know which people are likely to get promoted or demoted and whether a change is threatening to us. During these times we become speculative, worried, anxious and alert. Our emotions are warning us—that's their function.

This awareness is not limited just to us. Others pick up on our feelings with their intuitive radar. When we don't like someone, others know it. Let's imagine that we all acknowledge this uncanny ability and see how differently we'd behave. We would realize that all the "private conversations" we have about others are on some level known to them. Frightening, isn't it? We spend all this time avoiding difficult issues and we're dealing with them anyway, only covertly. (See Figure 2-2.)

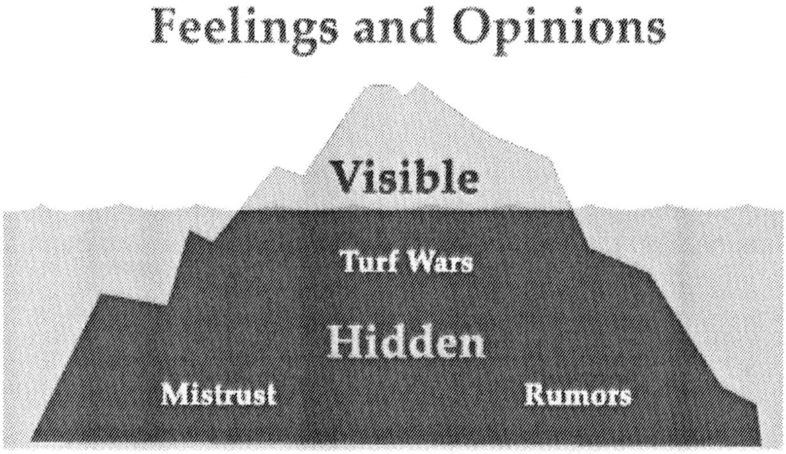

Figure 2-2: Feelings and opinions

Most of us pretend that we don't have this awareness. Instead we develop upset stomachs, headaches and heartburn. Even those who acknowledge these subtle feelings often don't have the courage or certainty to act on them. Our not-so-nice feelings are like a Pandora's box. We've been taught: "Don't open the box; don't *ever* open the box." Curiously, however, this is the very box we most need to open. And why not? The box is already open. We can hardly do more harm by releasing the hidden feelings.

False Beliefs About Business

Because emotions are so crucial to our success, why haven't we welcomed them into the workplace before now?

In business we have the illusion of rationality. We trust data charts and financial reports to tell us whether we're making progress. Yet research indicates that our feelings are significantly faster than our rational brains at sensing whether we're on track or not. We've worked hard to bring rationality into business and I'm not suggesting that we throw it out. We simply need to add the emotional component back into the equation.

Fear of Emotions

To understand how deeply embedded the idea of not sharing our feelings is, try to imagine an executive openly voicing one of these comments:

- "I felt left out when I wasn't invited to that meeting."
- "I am really scared about what this change means for me."
- "I feel unappreciated."
- "I was hurt by your actions."
- "I'm bored with my job and uninterested in my work."

It's hard to imagine anyone—much less an executive—expressing these feelings.

Whether we're employees, managers or executives, we've been taught from the time we were babies to suppress our true thoughts and feelings in order to be loved by those around us. At work, we're encouraged to express positive feelings but not negative ones. The cultural message is that feelings are too raw and primal and must be channeled into limited and acceptable modes of expression. We feel an instinctive danger, a fluttering in our stomach when we consider sharing our true reactions and feelings. Strong emotions of any kind make us nervous. People who are seemingly not in control of themselves make us nervous. We want them to "get a grip." We are afraid of emotions because we believe they are a force we can't control.

We believe that good business and emotions do not go together. We hold the following five erroneous beliefs about work that keep us from integrating emotions into our work practices:

Belief #1. Business is based on facts, not feelings. Business is logical. We make decisions based on facts. It's best to keep emotions out of it. We think: "This plan sounds great in theory but it doesn't feel right. I'd better keep quiet. I have no data to back up my opinion. People will think I'm disloyal."

Belief #2. If we address the issues we won't get anything done. It's a detour to talk about how we feel; we need to focus on the project. We think: "I realize that team members are upset about this decision, but I can't deal with this issue now or we'll miss our deadline. I don't have time to deal with everyone's reactions."

Belief #3. It's not safe to talk about what's really going on. We think: "It'd be politically incorrect to speak against this new project."

Belief #4. Our feelings are invisible to others. We think: "If I just keep my mouth shut, no one will know I'm upset about what's going on. I'll pretend that everything's okay."

Belief #5. We should focus on the positive, not dwell on the negative. We think: "No one likes a naysayer. It's best to look on the bright side of things."

The following beliefs shape our attitudes and behaviors toward emotions:

- *Emotions are inappropriate.* We are embarrassed to let others see our strong emotions.
- *Emotions are powerful.* We think we must acquiesce to others when they have strong emotions.

- *Emotions are invalid.* Facts are true but emotions are not to be trusted.
- *Emotions are uncivilized.* We don't know what to do or how to respond to emotions.
- *Emotions are lies.* We frequently deny what our emotions tell us.
- *Emotions are messy.* We resent the time and energy it takes to deal with emotions.

We think that we must *either* make good business decisions *or* address our feelings. It's an either-or proposition. So we either ignore the human needs and make good business decisions or we take the other person's feelings into account and neglect the tough business decisions.

Harnessing Emotions at Work

Emotions are a powerful force for action. They can be used to solve the problems we face. The word "e-motion" literally means "to move forward." Our feelings and opinions can be harnessed for the benefits they bring. Specifically, emotions can be used to:

- Improve communications. When emotions are part of our discussions, we achieve deeper levels of understanding and appreciation about the real issues.
- Find the underlying cause of problems. Emotions can lead us to the root cause of problems and help us resolve the real issues.
- Increase our ability to work as a team. Appreciating and respecting each other's feelings helps us work in greater harmony and get more done.
- Reduce interpersonal conflict. Even longstanding conflicts are resolved when emotional needs are honored and acknowledged.

- Enhance personal performance. When our feelings become part of the work equation, we are able to resolve our concerns and focus on the work at hand.
- Gain commitment to new initiatives. Expressing concerns and addressing our fears help us to fully commit to new initiatives.

Opening Pandora's Box

When we first open a Pandora's box, it is overwhelming and frightening. Gerry, a product manager in a software development company, wants to communicate the new corporate strategy to her employees. As employees learn about the strategy, it's painfully clear that they're angry about being left out of the decision-making process. They feel isolated and excluded from key decisions and many don't trust each other. Gerry is discouraged. Instead of embracing the strategy, employees are having a gripe session about the lack of leadership! She feels embarrassed to have these issues discussed so openly. She doesn't want to deal with her employees' frustrations. She thinks the entire session is taking a wrong turn.

What Gerry doesn't realize is that this discussion is a direct step toward employee commitment. Once employees express their doubts and fears, the discussion progresses to a positive tenor. They begin talking about the strategy and what they can do to implement it. Negative energy must be released before positive energy is available.

Emotional Energy is Fuel for Action

Emotional energy is fuel for action regardless of whether it's positive or negative. When our feelings are held back—such as when we think the boss is making a mistake, a peer is out to get us or a technical problem is being ignored—it's harder to feel enthusiastic and move forward. Emotionally, we have one foot on the brake. By ignoring unpleasant reactions we unwittingly smother the thing we desire most—emotional commitment and creative involvement. *When negative energy is suppressed, so too is positive energy.*

The Vital Bonds Between Us

Emotions are our "human bond" with one another. They connect us across races, economic barriers and social differences. We connect by sharing our fears, concerns and joys. Simply laughing together is a bonding experience. Tragedy and danger also unite us—when a death occurs and we rally around the employee to help; or a risky business venture requires us to work night and day against great odds to meet a deadline. We always remember these times. The feelings evoked are what build our relationships with each other.

At work we crave the feeling of aliveness that comes from honest relationships, but we don't trust the emotional vulnerability that's necessary to achieve it. To harvest the vibrant energies of hope, optimism, passion and commitment, we must also welcome frustration, despair, worry and fear. Our emotions are paired like Siamese twins that cannot be separated. If we want the one, we must also embrace the other. Welcoming the expression of emotions frees up enormous energy to focus on our collective goals.

Business Reality #2: Emotions impact how we feel, what we do and whether we're successful at work.

Success Action: Harness emotional energy to improve business performance.

Key Learnings

1. Precious time is wasted on hidden agendas, conflicts and mistrust at work.

3. To succeed, we need to learn how to work together.

4. We can simultaneously address emotional concerns and make good business decisions.

5. Positive and negative emotions are paired like Siamese twins—if we want one, we must also welcome the other.

6. Emotions are a powerful force for action.

7. Our feelings and opinions can be used to improve work relationships and effectiveness.

Chapter 3

Learn Facts About Feelings To Positively Affect the Bottom Line

It is not necessary to get away from human nature but to alter its inner attitudes of mind and heart.

J.F. Newton

In the conference room of a large architectural firm, two professionals, Juanita and George, are having a conversation over morning coffee.

Juanita: What's gotten into Jeff lately?
George: You noticed too?
Juanita: How could I help it? He has been moping around like a wounded puppy dog.
George: Yeah, ever since his "promised" promotion fell through.
Juanita: Do you think that's it? I'm not sure what's bugging him. All I know is that his attitude is really sour. Whatever happened, he isn't doing much work these days.
George: The worst of it is, he's dampening everyone else's enthusiasm about the upcoming trade show.
Juanita: You're right about that! It's no fun to be around him—he's so cynical—it's a pain to work with him.

Emotions Affect Job Performance

Juanita and George are dealing with emotional issues. They are stymied, not sure what to do and strongly affected by the dynamics that are taking place. Our emotional needs can manifest themselves as resentments, conflicts, retiring on the job, petty squabbles, emotional outbursts and sabotaging behaviors.

To understand the nature of emotions and how to cooperate with the feelings in ourselves and others, the following principles of emotions are important to keep in mind.

Eight Principles of Emotion

1. Emotional needs express themselves one way or another.
2. Negative emotions are an expression of need.
3. Our needs are not wrong or bad.
4. Emotions are the gateway to vitality and feeling alive.
5. We can address emotional issues and still "save face."
6. Immediate reactions to problems often disguise deeper feelings.
7. It is necessary to clarify individual needs before problem-solving with others.
8. We must express positive feelings and communicate negative ones.

Principle #1: Emotional needs express themselves one way or another.

To better understand our primal emotions and the dynamics at play, we can learn from the extremes of sex and violence that occur. Strong emotional reactions are the result of longstanding, frustrated needs. Violence can occur when emotions spill over. Sexual harassment and illicit affairs are grounded in unmet needs and emotional suppression. In hindsight, we can see how desperate we become when our human needs are denied.

While the majority of corporate workers handle the routine human indignities that come with employment, a very small percentage crack under the strain. Violence in the workplace was virtually unheard of before the first post office shooting took place in 1989. Since that time, acts of workplace violence have been increasing. Emotional tensions and fears can go underground and erupt into violence.

A Native American friend of mine spent nineteen years in prison for murder. Today he is a gentle marathon runner, an artist, a philosopher and a genuine spiritual teacher. One night we talked about the murder and how it felt to him. Listening to his story was difficult. The brutal, cold-blooded murder was an incredible high for my friend. I reacted with horror when he told me: "I have never felt so powerful! The day after, I felt exhilarated—like no one could touch me—like I would never die—like I was God. It was only later that the feelings of grief and sadness came."

All of his life he had been the underdog. As a Native American with little formal education and no money, he was treated frequently with disdain. In the act of murdering another human being, he became powerful. He desperately wanted to *be somebody*. He wanted to feel important. The only way he could get this feeling was to murder a stranger in cold blood.

Principle #2: Negative emotions are an expression of need.

Individuals who commit violent crimes are angry. I have learned much about emotions from Elleva Joy McDonald, in Minneapolis. We have talked about the problems caused by the rejection of anger. In one of our conversations Elleva Joy said to me: "We don't *like* anger—we don't accept it. We really don't know what to do with it, in ourselves or others. We think that all anger is 'fundamentally bad.'

But there are two kinds of anger. One kind of anger is good—we need it to survive. It's the anger that comes from our dignity rising up and shouting: 'No, I won't let you treat me like this! This is not right! No, I won't tolerate this anymore!' It's the part of us that propels us into action!"

We need this type of anger. Without it we are wimps—unable to rally to our defense, strike out in new directions and put an end to manipulative, abusive situations. It is necessary for survival—for our lives to be our own. *But we are terrified of it.* This is the anger that we must learn to accept.

The second kind of anger is unhealthy. It is utterly hopeless and despairing. At its core are bitterness and rage that come from the loss of hope. This is the anger that causes people to kill—themselves as well as others. The feelings are: There are no options left. Someone must pay. Something must happen. If I go down, you go down! Nothing is possible. Nothing is ever going to change! It's hopeless. I can bear it no longer.

Our anger does not have to be vented in self-destructive ways. It can be used to help us discover our needs.

Principle #3: Our needs are not wrong or bad.

The murder my friend committed was terribly wrong. *But his underlying needs and desires were not wrong!* His need was a human need, one that we all have: *the need to feel important.* All those years he spent waiting, wanting to feel important, and every day never getting it until one day, *hope was gone*. Then it was only a matter of time until his long-suppressed rage erupted into violence.

When acts of violence occur, it is not only the violent person who needs help. We see the perpetrator, but we must begin to understand how others and the organizational culture are involved. Where was the employee's manager when he or she felt so discouraged? What happened when the early alarms sounded their subtle signals? Why did everyone turn their heads and pretend not to see? Why didn't someone respond to the cries for help?

How often did the work culture suppress the expression of sadness, anger and even minor frustrations? How many times did the organization ignore the individual's or group's feeling of discouragement? How often did daily interactions leave people feeling inferior to others, if not downright worthless? How much did the harsh expectation that "everyone is responsible for their own problems" cause people to focus on work at human expense?

Principle #4: Emotions are the gateway to vitality and feeling alive.

Unmet emotional needs are linked not only with violent behavior, but also with inappropriate sexual behavior. Our sexual drives express pent-up emotional needs. Whenever we feel bored, pressured, tense, thwarted, restless, unfulfilled or disconnected, sexuality can be a ready vehicle for fulfillment. When emotional needs go unmet, they can show up in inappropriate sexual conduct.

A high-ranking executive of a large organization is in the process of getting a divorce. He feels a tremendous sense of loss. The business pressures on him are enormous. He desperately needs emotional support. He denies this need and the loneliness he feels at the top. With support no longer available at home, he looks elsewhere. He turns more and more to the relationship with his married administrative assistant for emotional support. She accompanies him on business trips. They have an affair. The situation causes enormous frustration in the organization because the woman is personally influencing his decisions! No one can access the president without going directly through his assistant. There is a lot of office gossip and resentment. His behaviors are detrimental, not only to himself but also to the organization.

In a different situation, an attractive female manager uses flirtation, innuendo and risqué body language to influence her male managers. Inside she feels insecure, but she covers these feelings with suggestive sexual behavior. In the short term, she gets the attention she wants—and maybe even the job assignment—but inside she feels undeserving of her success and even more inadequate and anxious. Her real need is to feel valued.

Desire to Feel Alive

Our needs become exaggerated when we work day and night in long meetings using only our brains and we don't acknowledge our need for laughter, movement, emotions and variety. We create a volatile situation. Then we eat too much, drink too much or misdirect our emotional energy. We want to feel *alive.* We want the safety of belonging and the warmth of intimacy.

Underneath the sexual, violent, abusive behaviors is the desire for personal vitality and connection with others. When these needs go unmet, some part of us *rebels*. Then our needs emerge in self-destructive ways. The alcoholism, abuse, misconduct and homicides are misguided, desperate attempts to meet our true needs.

Principle #5: We can address emotional issues and still save face.

Dwight, a customer service manager in an engineering firm, calls the local employee assistance counselor for help. He wants to fire Brad, a young employee, because he has made explicit sexual remarks to coworkers. At first Brad made "suggestive comments" to women, but after several warnings from Dwight, he stopped this behavior. Several weeks later, however, he started to be sexually aggressive with a male coworker. This is behavior that is *clearly unacceptable* in the working world! Brad has made a mistake that will not be tolerated.

Dwight wants advice about how to fire Brad without repercussion. The reason he called for help is because he is afraid. Brad has made several comments about owning a firearm and wanting to "blast some people away." This is one of the times when it's hard to value another human being. Dwight's initial plans for firing Brad are to hold a closed-door meeting, terminate him in the presence of three managers, have a police escort show him to the door, give him a box with the contents from his desk and send him on his way.

The counselor and Dwight talked for a long time before deciding what to do. Brad has a problem—a problem that is being acted out sexually. At some point in his life, he may have been sexually abused. The abuse issues may be rising to the surface and revealing themselves in inappropriate behavior. His actions are a cry for help.

It is not right for Dwight to ignore Brad's behavior. That would be the worst thing to do. Neither does he need to humiliate Brad for what he has done. Dwight chooses to fire Brad in a way that leaves his dignity intact. He is an excellent contributor and a hard worker, and Dwight tells him this. However, he has a problem that neither Dwight nor the organization can ignore. Brad is terminated and referred to a sexual abuse clinic. After the termination, Dwight stays in touch with Brad for several months to support his progress and job change. No violence results from the situation.

We do not want volatile or extreme emotions breaking out in the workplace. We know that without limits, boundaries and expectations about emotional control, relationships and work suffer. Social norms regarding behaviors exist for a reason. Our expectations of emotional control help us to:

- Reduce volatile reactions.
- Create an environment of safety.
- Provide balance necessary for our well-being.
- Ensure the stability of the group.
- Allow us to focus on tasks that need to be done.

However, completely suppressing our feelings keeps us from being in touch with:

- Work situations that are abusive to our well-being.
- Our larger goals and dreams.
- Seeing important clues in interactions with others.
- Recognizing unhealthful motives and con games.
- Appreciating our need for balance and connection.

If welcomed and used properly, our emotions are the literal doorways that can lead us out of dark, destructive work relationships and situations into clear inner and outer realities that are supportive of who we are and what we need.

Principle #6: Immediate reactions to problems often disguise deeper feelings.

Our initial emotional response to a problem is often not the same as the deeper feelings involved. Denise, a health care consultant, walks into her office one day and discovers that the contents of her desk are piled in the corner of her office. As she surveys the situation, she becomes angry. She thinks: Who would dump my stuff on the floor without asking me first! This is an insult. Someone is going to hear about this. Shortly thereafter, Denise's supervisor comes in and says: "An emergency came up and we must use your office for two weeks. I am sorry we had to move your office unexpectedly. I didn't have a chance to warn you, so I put your things together in the corner so you could move them easily."

Later that night Denise reflects on the incident and realizes that although her initial reactions were anger and indignation, her real feelings are hurt and fear that perhaps they do not really want her in this job.

We have four possible responses to the presence of strong emotions. We can run away, respond with anger and deny the importance and intensity of what we are really feeling. The fourth option that is available to us is to correctly identify our true feelings and use them to address the situation by sharing our concerns and asking for what we need. It takes courage to implement this option. (See Figure 3-1.)

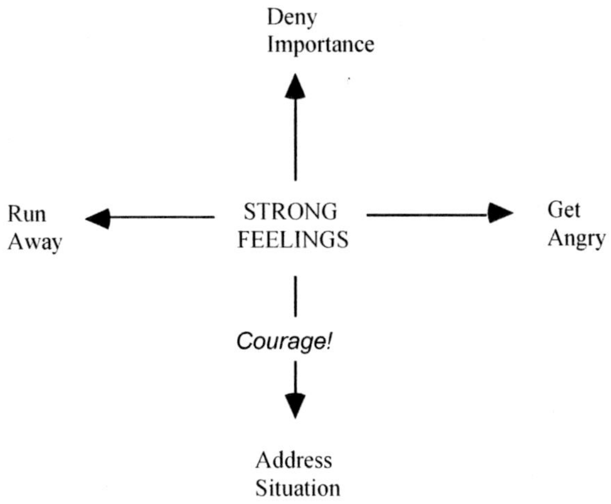

Figure 3-1: Reactions to feelings

Running Away From the Problem

A frequent response to intense feelings is to remove ourselves from the situation by avoiding others, not talking to them, moving to a new location or job, pretending the event never occurred, acting as if the person is not in the room. When a situation or person activates our deepest emotions, we may go to great lengths to avoid these feelings. At work, we avoid: confronting bosses, making presentations, working with specific individuals, tackling a technical problem, attending certain meetings, and controversial topics we need to discuss—all in an attempt to avoid the feelings that are activated by a situation.

Getting Angry

Anger, although it appears direct, is one of the strongest avoidance tactics we have because it keeps us away from our deeper, more vulnerable emotions. Outwardly, we seethe with resentment, yell at someone, stomp our feet, slam doors, make sarcastic remarks, talk behind the person's back or sabotage their success—all because we do not want to feel the emotions that are being activated inside of us. Anger frequently masks feelings of being hurt. It is safer to react with the brittle, harsh emotions of anger and resentment than it is to express the deeper, more vulnerable feelings of hurt, disappointment and sadness that are present.

Deny importance

When a person or situation hurts us in a significant way, we may attempt to diminish our strong feelings by rationalizing: This is not really that important. I am an "adult." This will blow over. I'll get used to it. They didn't really mean it. Sometimes we are able to forget about the incident and go about our business. But if the situation really bothers us, lingering resentment remains and minor incidents remind us of the very feelings we are trying to forget.

Observing Our Reactions

Our emotional alarms rarely come as a single feeling, but more often as a cluster of feelings. When strong emotions are present, it is not unusual for us to experience all three reactions to the same situation.

I remember observing my irrational responses to a friend's neglecting behavior. Initially I pretended that I didn't care and was not bothered by the behavior taking place. I am not a great pretender and was able to sustain my indifference for only a day. The next day when I thought about the situation, I felt angry and resentful and imagined myself lecturing, moralizing and delivering ultimatums about how "I should be treated better." Later that day, I entertained vivid fantasies of the person's leaving town so that I would never have to feel this way again. In a short period of forty-eight hours, I watched myself experience all three reactions to the feelings of hurt and insecurity. Even the most educated among us find ourselves reeling when people and circumstances activate our deepest hurts.

Addressing the Situation

To make the best use of primal emotions, we must move beyond initial reactions and claim our feelings before engaging in problem-solving with others. Until then, our actions, problem-solving and solutions are aimed at the wrong problem. In the earlier example of Denise, she could have easily responded by asserting her right to be treated differently or by pretending that the incident did not bother her. However, Denise decided to address her true feelings and take a different approach. She set up a meeting with her manager and asked for feedback on her performance. In the meeting she expressed her need to be assured about the value of her work. Explicitly addressing her need to feel valued was more beneficial to Denise than discussing the contents of her desk on the floor!

Solutions based on surface reactions never satisfy us because they do not respond to the heart of our concern. Many a lawsuit has been filed because of deep hurt activated by the way someone has treated us. Even when we win and there is financial remuneration, *there is still the feeling of not quite getting what we wanted.* True satisfaction comes when we identify, accept and respond to our deeper needs.

Principle #7: It is necessary to clarify individual needs before problem-solving with others.

It is a myth that we will ever become "mature enough" or "important enough" to stop having needs or caring if others like us. No amount of status and income can replace the joy and connection that we feel when we successfully bond with others. But to get this connection and keep it, we deny our feelings.

In a seminar on "Self-Empowerment," participants identified a problem in their work life. Next, they were told to write ten or more statements describing how they really felt about the problem. They were asked not to share these feelings with anyone because it might inhibit what they wrote! After participants completed the task, they described how it felt to write "unedited" statements. Participants made the following comments:

- "I feel guilty for having these thoughts."
- "I have never expressed these feelings before."
- "I hope no one sees this paper!"
- "I learned something new by doing this."
- "I think if I admit how I feel, I have to fix it."

The following statements block the expression of feelings in ourselves and in others. Notice the thoughts that are the most like your internal dialogue:

Communication Blocks:

- "Why don't I [you] just forget about this."
- "This is nothing compared to what someone else is dealing with."
- "If I [you] hadn't messed up, this wouldn't be happening."
- "Didn't I know this would not work out?"
- "Tomorrow, it will all be better."
- "I [you] must fix this situation."
- "I [you] must be a bad person."

To identify our genuine needs and claim them, we must allow our reactions and feelings to exist and not judge them. Knowing that we do not have to act on our feelings, express them to anyone or fix the situation frees us to be absolutely honest with ourselves.

Principle #8: We must express positive feelings and communicate negative ones.

The first challenge in using our emotional energy at work is to get in touch with the feelings that we experience. But getting in touch alone is not sufficient. The second step is to learn to express our feelings in such a way that they can be heard!

For some, getting in touch with emotions means relearning spontaneity and a childlike sense of wonder, getting out of our rational minds and allowing our feelings to blossom and be expressed. Many of us are overly analytical people who have lost our emotional spontaneity and immersed ourselves in structures of rationality and logic.

Others are too wanton and free with the expression of emotions and lack the discipline to discuss difficult issues with calmness and the necessary degree of rationality. For expressive individuals, getting in touch with emotions means learning to separate ourselves from negative feelings, detach and observe—instead of responding to every emotional cue and redirect emotional reactions into calm communication and the ability to listen to each other instead of taking things personally.

Once feelings are identified, they must be communicated so that others can hear them. If our purpose is to assess blame or seek revenge, we are not ready to talk constructively to the other person. It is important to express feelings so that they can be heard. Positive feelings can be expressed spontaneously. When we express positive feelings, we affirm our aliveness, enthusiasm and responsiveness as a human being. When these emotions are present inside us, we must sing them out or the music will stop. Unexpressed happiness dies on the vine, never bearing the wonderful fruits of enhanced worth and social bonding.

Some of us have *too many* words in our head and we miss the music; others of us have *too few* words in our head and fail to logically interpret or communicate our meaning.

As much as we like to feel good and share positive feelings, it is impossible to have long-term working relationships without experiencing negative feelings. Differences of opinion and conflicting needs are part and parcel of working closely with other people. When negative emotions are not communicated, they grow larger and more intense. Negative emotions are like a ferocious pit bull—the longer they exist without being acknowledged, the more they work up a frenzy internally. Anger denied eventually turns into rage; suspicions repressed develop into mistrust and blame; dislike ignored festers into cold hatred. We must communicate strong, negative emotions in ways that allow others to feel safe and not under assault. Anger carries with it blame and causes us to erect defenses or retaliate to protect our integrity.

The key to communicating negative emotions is *careful communication* rather than direct expression of these strong feelings. If I am angry about how you are behaving, I can either throw my anger at you or carefully communicate what I am feeling. Impulsive, unfocused expression of my feelings is a shock that will probably drive you away.

Value of Listening

Ironically, listening to the other person is the key to communicating our needs as well. When we listen, we help the other person clarify their feelings and needs. We also create a receptive environment for our needs to be discussed. Listening helps us to:

- Understand the situation better.
- Identify what the other person needs.
- Determine what we can do.
- Increase our ability to respond creatively.
- Stop defending our position.
- Gain cooperation from the other person.

Communicating about Problems

Too often we try to problem-solve with another person without understanding the real issues. To communicate to another person regarding a problem, follow these action steps:

1. **Affirm the importance of your working relationship.** "I would like to talk with you about an issue that concerns me. But first I want you to know how important you are to me

and how much I value our working relationship." Be specific about what you value. Say, "I value ______."

2. **Share your feelings.** "The other day, when ______ happened [be specific about the event], I felt ______ [describe your reactions and feelings]."
3. **Ask them to share their point of view and their feelings.** Carefully listen to their point of view, understand and summarize their response.
4. **Ask for what you need (be specific).** "What I want, need or would like to have happen is ______." Listen to and understand their response.
5. **Mutually agree on what to do in the future.**

As we accurately communicate our feelings about difficult issues and let others know that something is amiss in the flow of the relationship, we convey that a course correction is needed if we are to remain effective teammates and coworkers. We clear the path to productivity with our communication.

But I'm Not an Expert

We may feel uncomfortable with the task of dealing with emotions. All too often managers delegate the task of "dealing with emotions" to the human resource specialist. These professionals can become a crutch that allows managers to wash their hands of the situation. But the offices of the experts are too far away, the wait is too long, the response is too brief and the need is too great to leave emotional issues solely to the human resource professionals.

Managers and employees alike must become knowledgeable in handling human emotions. We must learn new ways to relate to each other—ways that acknowledge emotional needs; ways that include listening, caring and sharing, as well as the ability to set limits, encourage responsibility and say no. Our emotions can be the best teacher. The feelings and needs we honor in ourselves, we then understand and honor in others.

As we deal with emotions, we realize just how much they affect the success of our business everyday. Work relationships are strengthened or weakened by the existence of trust and teamwork. Feelings of skepticism or hope determine whether we are able to achieve a desired vision. The relationship between managers and employees determines whether individuals feel empowered or negated in their jobs. The ability to implement change is highly dependent on emotional harmony and commitment. The ability to contribute our best talents is determined by whether we feel safe from pending layoffs and recognized for our talents. The effectiveness of teams and communication across departmental lines is dependent upon managers having the skills to create synergy among groups and to welcome conflicting viewpoints.

As we understand the essence of emotions, we see that our emotions are like the elements of nature—sometimes raw, violent, changing and unpredictable; other times pleasant, warm, inviting and steady. Whether warm or cold, violent or steady—our emotions can be controlled but never completely tamed. Just as too much contact with the raw elements of nature is dangerous for us, neither is it healthy for us to completely succumb to our feelings. Similar to our need for contact with nature, we need to be in touch with our emotions on a regular basis, but not completely at their mercy.

Business Reality #3: What bothers us the most are the things we don't talk about.

Success Action: Learn facts about feelings to positively affect the bottom line.

Key Learnings

The Eight Principles of Emotion

1. Emotional needs express themselves one way or another.

2. Negative emotions are an expression of need.

3. Our needs are not wrong or bad.

4. Emotions are the gateway to vitality and feeling alive.

5. We can address emotional issues and still "save face."

6. Immediate reactions to problems often disguise deeper feelings.

7. It is necessary to clarify individual needs before problem-solving with others.

8. We must express positive feelings and communicate negative ones.

Chapter 4

Defuse Hot Buttons
To Reduce Conflicts at Work

Hating people is like burning down your own house to get rid of a rat.

Harry Emerson Fosdick

Stuart: Jake, have you finished that marketing report yet? I need it for a management presentation that's coming up. I hope it's ready.

Jake: Are you crazy? I'm up to my eyeballs in deadlines. There's no way I can get to that report.

Stuart: What! I was counting on you. I need that data for my report! This is a very important meeting. The VPs are coming from out of town and it's critical they get this information.

Jake: Here! [Jake tosses a file onto Stuart's desk.] The data's in here. Dig it out for yourself. You can get your hands dirty like the rest of us!

What Are Hot Buttons?

Volatile reactions occur when we activate each other's hot buttons. Hot buttons are intense emotional reactions to specific people, events or situations caused by personal vulnerabilities. Someone says or does something and our gut muscles tighten. We respond by closing up, striking out, withdrawing or yelling at them. It can happen in a second. In the earlier example, Jake's hot button is resentment. He feels he is doing all the dirty work and Stuart is getting all the glory.

Hot buttons are our instinctive reactions to situations that activate fear. *They are the consequence of past hurts more than present reality.* Hot buttons take place on a primal, survival level. We react instantly to events or people who threaten us. We believe that someone or something "out there" is making us angry and upset, not the feelings inside us. We have a brittle, fear-based reaction. Our jaws tighten, voices elevate, eyes widen and our movements become rigid and restrained. Everything in us contracts. We attempt to remove ourselves from these feelings by withdrawing, or blaming others. We hide from our vulnerabilities. The feelings connected with hot buttons are raw and difficult to face.

Research on the human brain sheds new light on these intense reactions. Our flight-or-fight responses are controlled by a part of our brain called the amygdala. The moment we sense that someone or something might be dangerous or threatening to us, the amygdala instantly tells our body "This is a crisis!" A flood of emotions overrides our rational thinking. Simply put, we can't "think straight" when we sense danger. Our responses aren't logical and the behaviors that follow make no sense.

Hot buttons differ from person to person. One person's hot button is triggered by a lie, another is triggered by the loss of an opportunity and still another is triggered by negative dynamics in a meeting. When hot buttons are activated, our responses go far beyond what's appropriate to the situation. We become rigid and tight and we lose our flexibility. The more intense our vulnerability, the hotter our reactions. Each of us goes to work with our uniquely tailored hot buttons. *Hot buttons cannot be removed;* they are part and parcel of what makes us who we are.

Situation #1

Matt, the supervisor of a production department, calls Jack, one of his foremen, into his office.

Matt: Jack, I want you to stop yelling at the employees on the line.

Jack: What are you talking about?

Matt: Last week, I had three complaints. You are coming on too strong and intimidating them. You've got to ease up.

Jack: I get the job done. No one is able to get these people to produce the results I do.

Matt: Jack, this is serious. You have to ease up. It could cost you your job if you don't. [Matt is utterly amazed with what happens next.]

Jack: My job! If *that's* what you're talking about, *I quit*. I don't need this crap. Catch ya' later.

Matt is stunned. Jack's resignation is completely unexpected. Jack's terrified that Matt will judge him as undesirable and unworthy. Jack can't tolerate being seen as a poor performer. When Matt's reprimand brings up these uncomfortable feelings, Jack's hot buttons are triggered. He goes from job to job rather than deal with the fear and shame he feels when confronted with his unacceptable behavior.

Situation #2

Steve is a successful internal consultant and works at the highest levels in the organization. However, he does not work well with his peers. Over lunch one day he talks with Janelle, another internal consultant:

Janelle: How's it going, Steve?

Steve: I'm exhausted. I worked all weekend summarizing the data I collected after four days of interviewing the executives. There's still so much to do. I have to eat and run so I can get ready for the president's staff meeting tomorrow.

Janelle: Can I help you in any way? I'm not as under the gun as you and it would be good for me to get some exposure to the leaders around here. Perhaps we could work on this project together.

Steve: No way! The executives wouldn't tolerate a new person coming in at this late date. I am the only one they trust. I can't let them down. Besides, I'm almost done with the report. Thanks anyway.

Steve feels inadequate unless he's seen as the brightest and most recognized person in his work unit. He sacrifices his weekends and himself in order to maintain his position of importance, then resents the lack of support from others. Steve's inner needs keep him from working collaboratively or receiving help.

Situation #3

We can know someone for years and never see his or her hot buttons. Then one day we say or do something that triggers them and fireworks go off.

Mary is a hard worker in a small law firm. She is known as the most gentle of people. She never gets angry and she helps everyone. For fifteen years she's successfully planned, anticipated and handled the administrative needs of five lawyers in a prestigious downtown firm. Last week Ric, one of the firm's newest lawyers, decided to hire Roxanne to help him complete a special assignment. Mary was hurt because she was not consulted about this decision.

Ric: Mary, can you come into my office for a moment?

Mary: Sure. Be right there.

Ric: I have a customer call coming in this afternoon. I want to brief you on the situation so you can get some information for me.

Mary: That would be fine but I won't be here this afternoon. Remember, you asked me to go down to the courthouse and retrieve information on the Jackson case. I'm planning to leave after lunch.

Jeff: Oh, that's right. I forgot. Oh well, call Roxanne. I'll ask her to do it.

Mary: [With a tight lip] Fine! I'll go get her. [Mary stomps out of Jeff's office, takes off her shoes and throws them, one after the other, at his head.] Mary's hot button has been triggered.

Situation #4

Chris, the information manager in a large medical facility, is frustrated with the performance of Bill, one of his programmers. He stops to talk about his concerns with Beverly, the human resource director.

Beverly: Hi, Chris. What's on your mind?
Chris: I'm concerned. It's about Bill. You know, the dark-haired guy who's kind of quiet.
Beverly: Sure, I know Bill. What's the problem?
Chris: Let's see. How can I describe this to you?
Beverly: Is he doing something that's bothering you?
Chris: Well, yes. He's always late. He does half the work my other programmers do and he doesn't fit in well with the group.
Beverly: Have you talked to him about this?
Chris: No, actually, I haven't. I was hoping you'd talk to him. I don't know what to say. Besides, I think he'd take it better coming from you. I know him too well.

Chris's hot button is fear of confrontation and the need to be liked at all costs. Chris grew up in a family where he wasn't allowed to express anger or disapproval of any kind. Now Chris avoids situations where he needs to confront others directly. He wants to be the one everyone likes, so he asks Beverly to take care of his problem.

The Effects of Hot Buttons

Every day we're surrounded by people we must work with closely. In confined spaces under tense working conditions, it's easy for coworkers to irritate one another. There are people whose very existence sets us off. We react strongly to their presence and conflict, suspicion and mistrust are just below the surface. We learn to walk around and sidestep these land mines. We avoid topics that might ignite others. Then one day dynamite goes off and we have no idea how things got so out of hand! Our hot buttons become tripwires that ignite conflicts when we step on each other's vulnerabilities. Emotional sparks go off long before our rational brain has time to figure out what's happening.

Dealing with hot buttons takes time and energy from the work that needs to get done. Hot buttons adversely affect business in the following ways:

- Individuals refuse to work with each other.
- Important communication does not occur.
- Decisions are made for the wrong reason.
- Power struggles take place.
- Projects are delayed or run over budget.

Hot buttons limit our options. When emotions take over, it's hard to consider options and change behaviors. Instinctively we feel danger and we move to protect ourselves. We insist on doing things our way, the way we've always done it before. It takes enormous courage to change our behaviors when we feel emotionally vulnerable.

Once I conducted an assessment for a client who didn't like female consultants. Given his reputation, my male colleagues suggested they present my findings to him. But I wouldn't hear of it. Their suggestion was a personal insult to me. As a child I grew up feeling dominated by an opinionated father, so one of my hot buttons is "being heard." I could not even consider their suggestion. Hot buttons limit our ability to respond and consider multiple options.

When someone or something activates our hot button, we don't want to be near them. More accurately, we don't want to feel the emotions seething within ourselves. We don't like being out of control, so we distance ourselves from the people, activities and circumstances that activate our hot buttons. We turn down risky assignments and shy away from volatile topics. Entire organizations and job assignments are restructured to avoid specific problems and people. The underlying issues are not addressed.

Our hot buttons go with us into every job, relationship and work experience that we have. Even after we've learned to recognize these reactions, they're still present and we're vulnerable to them. When tensions rise and fear surfaces, our hot buttons are the first emotions to respond.

Recognizing Hot Buttons

We can recognize hot buttons by their intensity and consistent presence in our lives. The following are indicators that we are dealing with a hot button. We continually:

- Complain and feel frustrated about circumstances.
- Wish we could be free of a person or situation.
- Obsessively try to figure out another person's motives.
- Plan endless strategies for dealing with a person or situation.
- Structure time so that we don't have to deal with a person or issue.
- Talk a lot to others about a person behind their back.
- Feel helpless and believe that nothing will work.

Hot buttons create predictable, almost scripted, reactions. Like a broken record we hear ourselves saying: "They don't appreciate me" or "I always take the blame" or "They never listen." When our hot buttons get pushed, we sing the same tired song over and over until we learn a different tune.

Keeping Hot Buttons from Taking Control

We need to learn new ways to deal with our hot buttons. If we don't, we're going to repeat the same conflicts. To defuse hot buttons we must recognize them and change ourselves. Short-term solutions such as taking a vacation from work may ease the situation, but lasting solutions require internal change.

We need to accept our role in the drama before tension dissolves. It's easier to blame others than it is to change ourselves. But this strategy won't bring peace.

To defuse hot buttons we must identify what we want and take responsibility for getting it. Asking others to meet our needs only intensifies our neediness because we can't control what they do. Rarely do we get what we want from others unless we are first giving it to ourselves. Our needs boomerang back to us so we can meet them.

Stop Reacting

The first step in dealing with hot buttons is to stop reacting and stop trying to change others. We must stop talking about the problem with others who sympathize with our cause, stop engaging in overt conflict and stop justifying our actions and why we are right. Without stopping this behavior we're still trying to gain the upper hand and get others to do what we want.

We must literally *stop* using our personal time and energy to think about the other person and what we are going to do next. We *stop* trying to get them to "be" or "do" what we want. This is very difficult. We don't want to stop. We don't think we should stop. Our first reaction to stopping is: "Yes, but this situation requires me to do something. There is no way I can just stand by and let this happen." We are afraid the other person might win or get by with something if we don't take action. After all, if we don't stand up for what's right, who will? We don't want to give up fighting for what we want. Stopping makes us feel helpless and vulnerable.

Withdrawal is a large first step. Part of us needs to keep the drama going. On an unconscious level we're *attracted to* the conflict. That's the nature of hot buttons—they are deeply embedded in our psyches. The idea of changing ourselves seems antithetical to what we're trying to achieve. In our clouded state of mind we know that *we* aren't causing the problem, *they* are. But the truth is, the only person we can change is ourselves. When we change how we feel, react and think, we increase the likelihood that others will change. *When we change, others change.*

Hot Buttons Affect A Management Team

Dick and Kathryn are the president and vice president of a research and development company. One of their products receives national acclaim for its innovative technology. The development work is complete, patents are in place and it's time to aggressively sell the new product.

Initially things go well. Kathryn and Dick have a long history of working together and respect each other's abilities. But as pressure mounts to get the new product out the door, hot buttons take control.

Dick is on the road every week and he is difficult to contact. Many decisions are delayed until he returns to give his input and approval. Dick likes to shoot from the hip and forms his opinions based on anecdotal data gathered from customers in the field.

Kathryn resents Dick for his views and thinks he doesn't listen to her. She wants Dick to value her marketing analysis that she works for hours to complete. When Kathryn disagrees with Dick, he gets angry and storms around the office. Dick resents Kathryn's need for detail and feels thwarted by her lack of enthusiasm for his ideas. Kathryn responds by taking control. Many days she feels the success of the company rests solely on her shoulders.

As their emotional needs intensify, the once-effective partners lose their ability to work together. Dick makes decisions to show Kathryn that she can't micromanage him. Kathryn ignores Dick when he contradicts her opinions. Staff meetings are unproductive. Communication and decisions are loaded with emotional tension.

Both Dick and Kathryn lose sight of the value they once saw in each other and begin to focus on each other's inadequacies. Both want the other to change. At the office they avoid each other in a desperate attempt to ease the tense situation.

The first step for Kathryn and Dick to take is to stop reacting and stop trying to change each other. For two weeks they declare a work zone that is free of confrontation. During this time Kathryn and Dick sort out their personal needs, beliefs and behaviors about the situation.

Accept Personal Responsibility

To defuse hot buttons we need to stop seeing the problem as *theirs* and start seeing the problem as *ours!* We start accepting our part by asking these questions:

- How am I contributing to this problem?
- What underlying beliefs and assumptions are influencing my behaviors and causing me to react so strongly?
- What do I really want in this situation?
- Why am I reacting so strongly? What fears and needs are driving my reactions?
- Is this situation similar to conflicts I've had in the past?

The first step is to see our part in the drama. Unless we recognize our part, we won't be able to change our behavior. Acknowledging our fears and changing our beliefs enables us to change our behaviors.

Kathryn and Dick decide what they really want. Dick wants to have his opinions and input from the field valued. Kathryn wants to feel less burdened by the demanding expectations she places on herself and others.

Both Dick and Kathryn decide to change. Dick starts to let others question his opinions without becoming reactive and defensive. Kathryn begins to relax her steely grip on responsibility and ask for help from Dick and her employees. Change does not come overnight. Slowly Kathryn and Dick replace their instinctive reactions with new behaviors. By changing themselves first, they improve both their relationship and business situation.

Changing From the Inside Out

All change requires personal change. Until we change ourselves, better results don't happen. If we want to lose weight, we must eat differently. If we continue the same old behaviors, the changes we desire will never happen. There's an old saying: "If you do what you've always done, you're going to get what you've always got."

To sustain new behaviors, we must alter our *internal* beliefs and attitudes. For example, if we eat to console ourselves, we must believe there are better ways to console ourselves. Aligning our beliefs and behaviors with the results we want is the key to all change. The faster we act in ways that are consistent with the results we want, the quicker change occurs.

Resolving Hot Buttons

To resolve hot buttons and achieve dramatically different results, we need to accept responsibility and initiate personal changes. In the following example Frank, the vice president of claims processing for a multinational insurance company, takes several steps to achieve radically different results.

Frank's division is losing money. Customer complaints are high, competition is heating up and expenses are out of control. No one knows how to stop the financial leaks and there are rumors the division is being sold. Clearly something needs to be done.

Frank decides to take on the challenge. He says, "I took this assignment as a personal challenge. No one wanted to look at the problems. I felt like I was rubbing managers' faces in cow pies to get them to talk about the issues. They didn't want to talk because it was *their* cows that made the mess."

Frank empowered a cross-functional team of employees to evaluate the situation and make recommendations. After extensive analysis, the team recommended a major reorganization. Upper management approved their recommendations and implementation began in earnest.

At this point the other division managers began to resist the change. Several managers did not like how the new structure affected their areas of responsibility. They started to undercut Frank's team and question top management's decision to restructure. Frank found himself at war with his peers and defensive about their recommendations. He described his personal reactions as "combative, defensive, controlling and highly protective of his team." For nine months he struggled. The other managers fought him every step of the way.

Frank finally hit the wall. He asked himself, "Why am I doing this? I'm completely burned out." Frank took time out to reflect on his situation. He was tired of fighting everyone, tired of doing it alone and tired of defending his staff. His work and personal life were completely out of balance. Hitting the wall was useful because it forced Frank to stop and ask himself, "What am I trying to achieve?" He realized he had gotten so caught up in the power struggles that he had forgotten his real objectives.

Frank accepted personal responsibility and asked himself these questions:

- "What do I really want?"
- "What are my goals in this situation?"
- "What is the best possible outcome?"

Frank knew the results he wanted. More than anything, Frank wanted his division to be profitable again. He also wanted his work life to be less stressful and more rewarding. He wrote down his desired outcomes:

- "I want the implementation team to succeed and help our division become profitable."
- "I personally want to feel more supported by the other managers."

Frank reviewed his beliefs and attitudes about the situation and wrote them down. He discovered these attitudes:

- "I think I'm right."
- "I don't trust the other managers."
- "I feel alone in this battle."
- "I don't think my staff members can stand up for themselves."
- "I feel like I'm the only one who cares."

Next, Frank honestly wrote down his behaviors:

- "I don't listen to the opinions of my peers."
- "I'm defensive about what we are trying to do."
- "I haven't involved other managers in the process."
- "I haven't allowed my staff to handle their own battles."

After reflecting on his situation, Frank realized that he wasn't listening to his peers or accepting their views. His attitudes and behaviors were highly controlling and not participative.

Frank decided to try out new attitudes and behaviors. He stopped being defensive and started listening to different points of view. Frank asked his peers for their opinions and started implementing many of their ideas. When opportunities arose, he shared his strategies with them. He stopped forcing his solutions down their throats and spent time helping them understand his strategies.

Over time the changes in Frank's behavior paid off. He started feeling better about work and had more energy. He stopped seeing his peers as "the enemies." He discovered that the other managers had many good ideas that he hadn't considered. Tensions eased. His life came into balance. Frank's team was able to successfully implement the new organizational structure. When Frank changed, his peers became more receptive to his ideas.

Three Steps of Accountability

Take time to apply the Three Steps of Accountability to your work situation. Identify a specific situation that frustrates you. Use the following questions to sort out your attitudes and beliefs about this situation. Identify specific changes you can make in your behaviors and attitudes and begin implementing these changes. Evaluate the results over time and see if you are getting the results you want.

First step: Identify the results you want.

- What's happening now?
- What do I wish were different in this situation?
- What do I really want?
- What are my goals in this situation?
- What is the best possible outcome?

Second step: Evaluate your current beliefs and attitudes.

- What are my beliefs about this situation?
- What attitudes do I have about the situation?
- What assumptions are driving my behaviors?

Third step: Initiate new behaviors and evaluate the results over time.

- What behavior am I willing to change?
- What new behaviors will I implement?
- When will I evaluate the results of my behaviors?

Lasting results do not happen immediately. You must continue the new behavior for a period of time. After two or three months ask yourself, "Are my behaviors bringing me closer to the results I want?" If not, go back and identify new behaviors. New behaviors will always produce different results.

Actions You Can Take

The following activity will help you discover actions that you can take to change frustrating situations you encounter at work. Complete this exercise and identify actions that you can take immediately to improve a difficult situation:

1. Identify a situation at work that bothers you. Select one where you feel that someone else is mostly to blame. Write the name of the situation in the line above the box (Figure 4-1).

   The name of the situation is this: ____________________

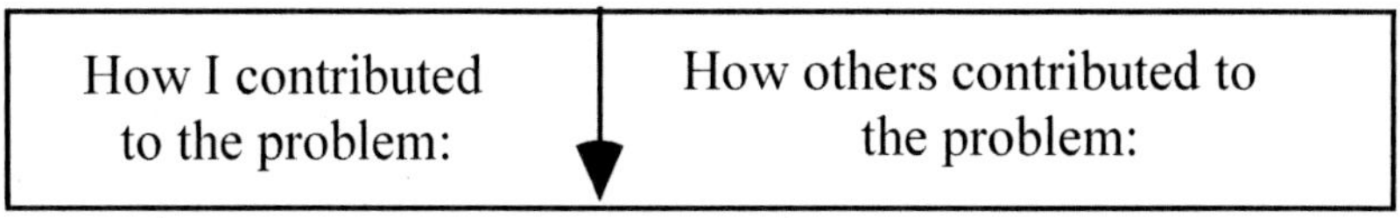
How I contributed to the problem:
How others contributed to the problem:

Figure 4-1: Who contributed to the problem

2. Draw a vertical arrow inside the box to indicate the degree to which you feel responsible for the problem. *Note:* If you feel mostly responsible, draw the arrow toward the right side of the box. If you feel less responsible, draw the arrow toward the left side of the box.

3. Under the left side of the box (Figure 4-2), write specifically how you contributed to the problem (I forgot..., I neglected..., I assumed...). Now, under the right side of the box, write specifically how others contributed to the problem (they did..., said..., forgot..., denied..., made..., hurt...).
   Note: At this point you have a description of who did what to create the problem.

How I contributed to the problem:	How others contributed to the problem:

- I did…
- I thought…
- I said…

- They said…
- They did…
- They forgot…

Figure 4-2: How problem was created

4. Now repeat this exercise on the same incident and assume responsibility for the entire box (Figure 4-3). This is challenging, but try to do it. Write down all the things that you *could have done* to prevent the problems listed in the right column.

How I could have prevented this problem:

- What I could have said…
- Where I could have looked…
- What I could have stopped…
- How I could have responded…

Figure 4-3: Assuming personal responsibility

Once you have completed this exercise, take a moment to realize how many actions you could have taken to prevent the problem from happening. When negative things are happening, we don't realize all of our choices.

When you are facing a problem, ask yourself these three questions to identify what you can do to take responsibility:

- What can I do to change this situation?
- How can I take constructive action?
- What do I need to let go of because I can't control it anyway?

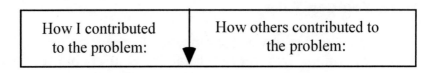

Author's note: I am indebted to John Enright in San Francisco, California, for the previous activity.

Defusing Hot Button Activities

The following are additional actions you can take to reduce the effects of hot buttons:

- Learn to observe your hot button reactions without judging them. Write them down. Use these statements to discover your hidden needs and beliefs.
- Try exaggerating your reactions in private—really overdo it. Enjoy! Pick a friend who laughs with you, not at you.
- Find easy ways to connect with "your adversary." Stop by his or her desk and ask for a paperclip. Any "neutral" behavior that makes a connection will do. Do this once a day until it becomes comfortable.
- Begin to say positive things about this person to others. You will be amazed how well this works to change your attitude and theirs.
- Practice "emotional Tai Chi." When the person says or does something that throws you off balance, learn to flow with your reactions rather than tensing up. This response takes practice but is gratifying when you can do it.
- Stop talking to other people about the problem or the person. Avoid people who keep the fight going or enjoy your complaints. Hang out with people who encourage you to talk about *yourself*, not about the other person.
- Draw a picture that illustrates the current situation and your reactions. Stick figures work well. Then draw a picture of how you want the relationship to work. Enjoy! This is a fun and very powerful change technique.

When it Doesn't Work Out

Sometimes no matter what we do, there's no good solution. The tensions and differences run too deep to resolve them. When this happens the only solution is to stop trying and ask yourself these questions:

- Why am I here?
- What is my purpose in this job?
- What can I achieve in this situation?
- Can I accept the situation as it is and contribute what I can?
- Are the dynamics so painful and disconcerting to me that I need to find another job or role in the organization?

Arm wrestling and psychic warfare take a heavy toll. Realize that some situations are simply not workable and move on.

Summary

Business relationships are a lot like marriages. In the beginning the romance of what's possible is strong enough to hold things together. But as the reality of working together takes place, hot buttons emerge. Most of our conflicts are born out of our desire to *get someone to behave differently toward us.* As long as we're dependent on another person to act differently, we're going to be disappointed. Demanding that someone change is like asking for a present—we may or may not get it.

Hot buttons can be managed. It's our job to know what sets us off and to ask for what we need. Others may or may not respond. Instead of seething, grumbling or erupting, we can change ourselves or leave the situation. Peaceful, lasting solutions are within our reach.

Business Reality #4: Conflicts and resentments thwart good business performance.

Success Action: Defuse hot buttons to reduce conflicts at work.

Key Learnings

1. Hot buttons are caused by past hurts more than by present reality.

2. Hot buttons limit our ability to consider multiple options.

3. When conflicts erupt, hot buttons are the first emotional reactions.

4. Asking others to meet our needs only intensifies our neediness because we can't control what others do.

5. The first step in dealing with hot buttons is to stop reacting and stop trying to change others.

6. When we change, others change.

Chapter 5

Address Hidden Dynamics To Improve Business Decisions

Men are but children of a larger growth.

John Dryden

Are your business decisions being undermined by hidden emotional dynamics? The following are examples of situations where hidden dynamics are interfering with performance and results.

Skepticism Undermines New Venture

Jake is hired to launch a new business venture. His background and skills are unique and greatly expand the services offered by the company. Jake is working on the "product of the future" that will lead the company into new markets. However, the new product requires faster response time, higher levels of service, a longer sales cycle and in-depth knowledge of the customer.

The old guard is skeptical about what Jake is trying to achieve. They don't understand the new business and secretly harbor doubts about its success. The managers keep Jake out of their accounts, fail to show up for his meetings and place his requests at the bottom of their priority lists. They are afraid—afraid that Jake's project will take away money from their budgets, interfere with their accounts and possibly succeed, thereby forcing them to change the way they are doing business.

Jake feels isolated and disconnected. He senses the lack of support for the new venture and believes his talents are not being appreciated. The support and encouragement he needs to launch the new product do not exist. Jake becomes discouraged.

Every day the situation erodes his self-confidence and makes him wonder if he should even be there. At home, he talks to his wife and friends, but at work the real issues are not addressed. Mistrust and fear prevent Jake and his company from succeeding with the new venture.

Symptoms of Hidden Dynamics

How do we know if hidden dynamics are influencing our business decisions negatively? Endless decision loops indicate that emotional needs are interfering with making good business decisions. One manager described it this way: "We meet and talk endlessly about options and possibilities, but we don't seem to reach any conclusions. The decisions we make never go anywhere. We can't implement once we decide. We can't make anything happen."

Confusion is inevitable when business decisions and emotional needs collide. The issues run together and every decision becomes complicated and difficult to implement. These dynamics frequently show up in family-owned businesses, business among friends and romantic relationships at work. It's not that these types of relationships can't work. It's that, in these types of relationships, we are vulnerable to confusion.

When hidden dynamics are present, we tend to:

- Tread lightly around certain issues or avoid them altogether.
- Hesitate to suggest specific solutions.
- Try many different solutions, but none of them works.
- Bitterly complain, but feel unable to take action.
- View new options as too complicated to implement.
- Hope that things will change and improve.
- Feel trapped between a rock and a hard place.

Individuals in these dynamics either feel smothered, controlled, anxious and unappreciated or they feel frustrated, angry, and overworked. All parties feel unable to change the situation.

Nothing can change until the underlying emotional dynamics are acknowledged and addressed.

The following are examples of hidden dynamics at work:

1. Rumors Destroy a Group's Performance

When we don't talk openly about our concerns, rumors and speculation can destroy group trust and morale. A manager recruits a woman to fill an important management position. The manager and the woman are longstanding friends and there's an obvious bond between them. The employees feel envious when they see their manager giving special attention to the new employee. Suspicions and rumors begin to fly. Employees ask, "Why did he really hire her?" and "Are they having an affair?" Every time the manager and new employee meet behind closed doors or go to lunch, word spreads like wildfire. No one talks directly to the manager about their perceptions. Enormous time and energy are spent speculating about this relationship. But the deeper issues of jealousy and favoritism are not addressed.

When an outside consultant is brought in to deal with the group's "morale problem," the real issues surface. The manager and employee are not having an affair, but they frequently seek each other's company for solace and support. As a result of the intervention, the manager comes to realize that all of his staff members need more attention from him.

The hours of conversations and suspicions caused by the false assumptions in this situation cannot be underestimated. Enormous energy was wasted because no one could talk openly about their concerns or the real issues.

2. Mistrust Prevents an Important Change

An improvement team worked for months to find the fastest, most accurate way to process customer orders. They analyzed the work process, brainstormed options and identified solutions that would eliminate duplication and cut processing time in half.

But as they talked about their ideas, a sense of futility and despair filled the room. No one was excited about the likely outcome. What was wrong? Why such discouragement?

Their solution involved reassigning responsibility for paperwork from field support people to home office personnel. The change made logical sense, but team members knew there was so much distrust between the field sales people and home office people that the idea was bound to fail. Home office employees didn't trust field sales to give them accurate information; field sales didn't trust home office employees with their accounts. Lack of trust was the real issue. For the new idea to succeed, trust needs to be developed between these two groups.

Without trust that comes from honest communication, the best plans in the world can fail. Trust is built on the belief that "I can count on you to do what you say; I can depend on you." When we don't have trust, we create elaborate mechanisms to ensure, verify and monitor the behavior of other people or we avoid working with them altogether.

3. Emotional Ties Thwart Good Decisions

Ten years ago, two brothers and four of their friends started a business together. Each left a larger company, mortgaged their house and bet their future on each other's capabilities. The company succeeded beyond their wildest expectations. As the business grew, two members of the original six took a position in the field and the other four took positions in the home office. All served on the board of directors.

Tensions among them grew as differences of opinions arose between home office and field managers. Because of their original bond and the hardships they had been through, they avoided the conflicts they had with one another. Eventually, watered-down decisions undermined their business success. Shared history and emotional ties kept these managers from making good business decisions.

4. Greed Destroys a Business

Phil, Derrick and Bernie decided to start a business together. They struggled at first, but after a few years they had a profitable enterprise. Phil was contacted by a larger corporation interested in acquiring the company. He became excited and dollar signs floated before his eyes.

Phil decided to share this exciting news with Derrick but not with Bernie. As the two partners talked, they daydreamed about the profits from the sale of the business. Soon they rationalized why the money should go to just the two of them. Phil and Derrick met with Bernie and told him that he "wasn't cutting it" and they wanted to redeem his shares of company stock. Bernie was shocked. Sure, there had been tensions among them, but this was an unexpected blow.

Several weeks later Bernie discovered the paperwork proposing the sale of the company. He was furious. He sued Phil and Derrick and they ended up paying enormous legal fees to protect their right to sell the company. In the end, the other company decided not to buy the business and the young company went bankrupt. Greed destroyed this business.

Greed is one of the toughest emotional issues to deal with. Greed is the desire to take more than our share. No matter how much we have, it never seems enough. Greed can take the form of hoarding projects, withholding information or protecting political contacts so we can feel important. Amazingly, many are able to pull it off.

Greed is subtle and consumes us before we know it. When greed rears its head we *immediately rationalize* that what we are doing is "okay." We are willing to do almost anything to get what we're after. The ends justify the means, shabby motives are dressed up in lofty language, agreements are made in secret and we play close to the vest and try to beat our opponents. We can recognize greed in others, but almost never in ourselves.

Greed is a desperate need to have something outside ourselves to make us feel important. Greed is the ultimate con man of our vulnerabilities. In business, we silently condone the grabbing behaviors of greed. We even encourage them. To stop greed, we must first acknowledge the emptiness inside before it is possible to change our behaviors.

Stop Emotional Needs From Calling the Shots

Decisions about strategy, priorities, direction and allocation of resources are not effective when emotional needs are calling the shots. Our denied emotions show up as hidden agendas and adversely influence business decisions. Decisions are undermined when personal motives are to:

- Gain power and control.
- Delay a change that is threatening.
- Advance a specific project.
- Avoid exposure of a mistake.
- Sabotage another's success.

When decisions are motivated by personal agendas, the results are incorrect priorities, mistrust and interdepartmental warfare.

Addressing Hidden Dynamics

To address hidden dynamics, we must learn to separate our emotional needs from the business decisions—and address both. Emotional needs are the domain of the child within us. When our emotional needs are in charge of running the business, it's the equivalent of letting a child drive the family car. It's simply not a good idea. Business decisions such as deciding which products to offer must be based on customers' needs, not on whether we like the person proposing the new product. Job openings need to be filled by the person best qualified for the position, not because we owe someone something.

Today the scale is tipped too heavily either toward making bottom-line decisions or, conversely, toward responding to emotional needs. We don't know how to achieve the proper balance between these two dimensions.

We cannot thrive if we negate emotions; neither can we prosper if we totally succumb to emotional needs. As adults, we must have the wisdom to simultaneously address emotional needs and make good business decisions.

Take the case of Allen, a corporate executive who must sell off a portion of his business. This decision is agonizing for Allen because he values his employees and doesn't want to disrupt their lives. But the truth is that Allen can do both—sell the business and help his employees through the transition. At first, addressing both areas feels awkward—it's a bit like patting our heads and rubbing our stomachs simultaneously. We're not used to handling both dimensions at once. To harness emotional energy we must *simultaneously make good business decisions and address emotional needs.*

Feeling Trapped

If you are dealing with emotional issues, realize that the dynamics may be too volatile and entrenched to address by yourself. Resolving the problem requires new behaviors and decisions that the current structure may not allow. What is sometimes needed is a trusted outside person to guide you through the process. Trust is important because the existing dynamics will pull you back into the old, ineffective ways of operating. The following are guidelines for selecting a consultant to help you. Make sure that the consultant:

- Is a neutral third party.
- Is not perceived to be on anyone's side.
- Has credentials and a background in psychology.
- Has experience in business decision-making.
- Has no bias about the decisions the group should make.
- Expects the group to openly address the issues.
- Has the reputation of maintaining confidences.
- Does not create indefinite dependency.

Releasing ourselves from entanglement requires changing the game. As we start to do this, it feels quite unsafe. We must act in ways that upset old patterns and shed new light on the situation that exists. The *real* danger is remaining in the management quagmire. Group meetings and decision points become sinkholes that drain vital energy and attention away from work that needs to be done. Eventually, implosion occurs and someone leaves, relationships end or the company folds. Then everyone loses. I have seen and experienced the danger of this cycle and know its allures, false promises and destructive endings.

It is possible to change these dynamics without destroying the company or doing irrevocable harm to relationships. It is gratifying when the dynamics gradually change and individuals are able to perform again. The business issues and emotional needs must slowly be unraveled and each one addressed with integrity and care.

Separating Facts From Feelings

The following are steps that you can take to separate business needs and emotional needs:

1. Acknowledge the presence of strong feelings.
2. Clarify individual feelings and needs.
3. Separate personal needs from business needs.
4. Identify and respect the needs of the business.
5. Be willing to change based on what you learn.
6. Believe that a win-win solution is possible—for you, for others and for your organization.
7. Be truthful and compassionate with each other.

1. Acknowledge the presence of strong feelings.

The key to unraveling the situation is to *separate the emotional needs from the business needs.* Begin the process by acknowledging that a problem exists. Agree to meet on a regular basis to discuss the issues and make decisions about the best course of action to take. Give yourself uninterrupted time to do this. The first step is to admit there's a problem and agree to address it.

2. *Clarify individual feelings and needs.*

To unravel the present, you must revisit the past. In the past are unmet expectations, hurts and outdated agreements that need to be addressed before you can move forward. In this step, it is helpful to draw a time line and discuss the changes that have occurred in the organization. All members of the team share in the re-creation of history that has taken place. This step is an essential building block that enables group members to understand how group dynamics and company priorities evolved. Using the time line, individuals take turns describing how they came to the organization. Each person describes their initial expectations about what they could contribute to the organization and what they would receive in return. Initial expectations often set the stage for later developments.

3. *Separate personal needs from business needs.*

Discuss how the past is influencing the present situation. At this point the difficult issues are discussed. Individuals talk about expectations that have not been met, disappointments along the way and mistrust that has developed over time. Each person tells his or her own story uninterrupted by others except for questions. Once personal needs, disappointments and expectations are openly shared, individuals are more willing to accommodate what needs to be done from a business point of view. Avoid problem-solving at this point.

4. Identify and respect the needs of the business.

It is now time for the group to focus on the needs of the business. The key issues and priorities of the business are agreed upon. Next, the group members list the areas of concern and together select one of these areas to address. Many of the former disputes will be seen from a new perspective and with greater understanding because of sharing that took place in the earlier steps.

5. Be willing to change based on what you learn.

Decisions are now made to address the business situations and personal needs. Roles may be altered, projects may be dropped, new structures may be put in place or the decision-making process may be changed.

6. Believe that a win-win solution is possible—for you, for others and for your organization.

The sixth step is the easiest because managers know how to take action. After decisions are made, the group develops action plans that reflect their decisions and determine who will do what by when.

7. Be truthful and compassionate with each other.

The most challenging part of this process is to trust each other and to tell the truth. The review of the history is critical because it places individual needs in a larger context and increases trust and understanding among team members.

Statements that Address Hidden Dynamics

When you are faced with hidden dynamics, the following statements can be used to ask for a change:

- "I am not comfortable with the decision that is being proposed. I'm concerned about the results. Can we talk about what we're trying to accomplish?"
- "There is a lot of speculation and conversation going on behind closed doors about this issue. I wonder if we might talk more openly about our real concerns."
- "I receive a lot of verbal support for this project, but no one shows up for my meetings, wants to spend time on the project or indicates much interest. Can we talk about what you are really thinking?"
- "You seem worried. Is the pending reorganization [or decision, change, etc.] bothering you?"
- "We used to get along well, but once I was promoted to supervisor, all of that changed. I was wondering if we might have a cup of coffee and talk about how we both feel and get things back on track."

The following is a list of actions you can take to respond to the hidden dynamics affecting your work effectiveness:

- Refuse to talk about a problem unless the people directly involved are in the discussion as well.
- Set up a meeting and invite all parties to come and share their views openly.
- Refuse to spread rumors or speculate about unverified information.
- Ask direct questions about suspected motives and hidden dynamics. For example, "Do you want my job?" "Do you disagree with the decision?"
- Publish questions and rumors in the weekly newsletter and counter them with facts.
- Invite employees to talk openly about the rumors that abound. Then have an open discussion about the issues and concerns that are on people's minds.
- When important decisions are being made, invite people to openly acknowledge heretofore unexpressed concerns.
- On a regular basis, set aside a special time for people to share their questions and concerns. This simple checking-in procedure will stop rumors before they spread.

Implications

I have described just a few of the situations that are caused by hidden dynamics in the workplace. To address these issues we need to recognize and set aside our egos and resentments that come to work with us.

The question becomes: How will we choose to deal with the real issues on our minds? Will we deny them, ignore them, pretend they don't exist—and let them play themselves out under the table? Or will we acknowledge them, discuss them and resolve them openly? Are we willing to move through our discomfort and uneasiness? Are we willing to take the risks involved? Are we willing to listen to others? Are we willing to speak up for ourselves? Will we go beneath the surface to find out what is really there? As the old miners used to say, "There's gold in them there hills!" But getting to it can be messy. Are we willing to dig and find it?

Business Reality #5: Up to fifty percent of time in an organization is wasted due to mistrust.

Success Action: Address hidden dynamics to improve business decisions.

Key Learnings

1. Hidden dynamics thwart good business decisions.

2. The drive for power creates many hidden agendas.

3. Greed is the ultimate con man of our vulnerabilities.

4. Past history and emotional ties can keep business leaders from making good decisions.

5. We need to separate emotional needs from business needs and address both needs.

6. To improve the present, we must sometimes revisit the past.

Chapter 6

Drive Out Fear
To Promote Exceptional Communication

Anyone who has begun to think places some portion of the world in jeopardy.

John Dewey

Why is it that good news travels up—and bad news sinks like a stone?

Fear is at the heart of our communication problems. We're afraid to confront authority, afraid of reprisal, afraid of being vulnerable and afraid of losing control. Fear exists at all levels. According to one study, seventy percent of employees are afraid to speak up for fear of repercussion. Decades of cultural conditioning are at work here. We've been taught by word and deed not to challenge the people at higher levels. The very fiber of our work culture is built around agreeing with the person in charge, even if that person is wrong.

Nathan, a top executive in an insurance firm, ties his career to a new product. The product is in trouble—customers are complaining and profits are dropping. In desperation Nathan hires an outside firm to identify the problems and recommend solutions.

The consultants find significant problems. Customer service for the product is inadequate, the sales force doesn't know how to sell it and the computer system needs to be significantly upgraded to handle the product information. To make matters worse, many of these issues were identified three years ago by the sales force, but personnel at the home office didn't listen.

Upon hearing this report Nathan is livid. He says to his staff, "This is the worst report I've ever seen." Then he asks, "Does anyone agree with this report?" Of course, they all say "No." He fires the product manager, fires the consultant team and discredits the findings as being ludicrous.

Nathan is afraid. He's afraid of failure—the opposite side of his equally strong desire for success. His fears make it difficult to hear bad news—even when he asks for it. Any manager who dares to confront Nathan is in danger of losing his or her job.

When we're afraid we don't want to hear other perspectives. Bad news carries an implicit judgment that threatens us. If something we care about is "bad," we think that we must be "bad!" These are the wages of fear—and no one is immune. Fears cause blow-ups, suspicion, blame and defensiveness. Executives are as likely to be afraid as front-line employees are.

In a consumer product group a top-level manager invites employees to speak with "more candor." The unanimous reaction by employees is, "No way!" A single invitation from management can't undo decades of programming to the contrary. Despite open-door policies, there are multitudes of problems and feelings that employees will never share.

Fear of Conflict

Fear keeps us from addressing interpersonal tensions and performance issues. I've seen managers literally get sick to their stomachs before going into a team-building session where they're going to discuss the issues they have with each other. Addressing unmet expectations, personality conflicts, betrayals and opposing points of view is hard for us. We learn early in life to avoid these difficulties. By the time we're adults we are adept at ignoring what bothers us. However, good working relationships require that we talk openly about what we want and need from each other.

Roger, a bank president, avoids a performance issue with one of his managers, Frank. Roger promoted Frank from a sales management position into the human resource position. Frank had no background or experience in human resources but he wanted the job.

After the decision was made, Roger realized he'd made a terrible mistake. Roger didn't want to hurt Frank's feelings, so he avoided the issue. For six years the organization worked around the fact that Frank was an inept human resource manager. No one was happy about the situation. Eventually the concerns became too great to ignore.

Roger developed a plan. He asked his staff to go through career testing to identify their strengths and weaknesses. Next he called a team meeting to discuss the results. In this meeting Roger used peer feedback and the assessment information to remove Frank from his position. Under the guise of a feedback session, Roger "restructured" the job away from Frank. Roger told Frank that the decision was based on the assessment and peer feedback. Not once did Roger talk to Frank about his lack of skills as a human resource manager.

In business Roger is able to "leap tall buildings in a single bound." Yet with his direct reports he can't discuss performance issues or make the changes needed. He tries everything—except telling the truth.

Pressure to Conform

Fear causes us to conform. Conforming is when we give up what we know is right in order to fit in with the group and be accepted. Consider the following statements and the messages they send:

- "Do what you're told."
- "Don't rock the boat."
- "Fit in—be a team player."

We send these messages to each other overtly and covertly. The underlying directive is: don't make waves, obey the rules, fit in. Unfortunately, what we get for our efforts are watered-down decisions and poor choices.

Standing up for what we believe is difficult. We don't get brownie points for being the organizational irritant. Mavericks are exalted in the movies, but in real life they're thrown out. It's one thing to root for a fictional character who bucks the system; it's quite another to risk the livelihood you need to feed your family. We conform not because we're weak but because everything we have is at stake. Our ready compliance with the majority leaves us with lackluster and sometimes disastrous decisions. When fear is present we:

- Hesitate to share our ideas.
- Resist the unexpected.
- Follow the rules.
- Take feedback as criticism.
- Watch our back side.

When we feel safe and supported in our relationships, we're able to:

- Freely contribute our ideas.
- Explore innovative solutions.
- Listen to feedback.
- Speak up when we disagree.
- Learn from mistakes.
- Adapt to change faster.

Why Are We Afraid?

At the heart of fear lies our need to be valued as human beings. The thing we fear most is rejection. Our conflict-ridden behaviors come from deep fears about not being accepted. Our need for acceptance is like a pebble that gets tossed into a pond and quickly drops out of sight and all we can see are the waves that ripple out. The pebble itself disappears. (See Figure 6-1.)

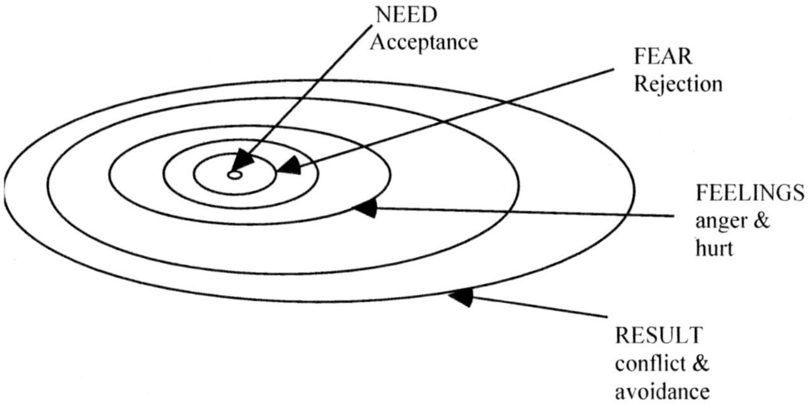

Figure 6-1: The ripple effect

When a negative incident occurs, fear is our first reaction and the waves of anger and hurt expand from there. Imagine learning that a coworker is complaining to your boss about a mistake you made. What's your reaction?

We react because we feel our worth as a human being is being questioned. More than anything, we fear rejection. So we protect ourselves at all cost. The end results are lawsuits, turf wars and interpersonal conflicts. To get to the bottom of it all we must go for the pebble. We must *know* that it's the pebble of acceptance we are looking for and not let ourselves get distracted by the reactions.

The Ripple Effect

The following are two examples of what happens when our core needs are threatened and the ripple effect starts.

Example #1:

Madeline, a project manager, consistently underestimates the cost of projects and overruns her budget. Her boss is furious about the overruns and starts to micromanage Madeline. Madeline reacts and thinks: I won't share any more information than I'm asked to share; I hate being micromanaged. Her boss labels Madeline as uncooperative and untrustworthy. *Madeline's real need is to be seen as a worthy contributor.*

Example #2:

Eric's manager decides to reassign some of Eric's favorite work to a different person. Eric is disappointed and thinks: My manager isn't looking out for me; he doesn't like me; I'm going to stop contributing in meetings. Eric's manager thinks he's uncooperative and not a team player. *Eric's real need is to feel that his contributions are valued.*

In these examples, notice how each person's reaction makes the situation worse. Our negative reactions and self-talk begin as soon as we think someone has damaged our self-worth. When we don't feel valued and appreciated, conflicts and resentments are likely to escalate.

Action Exercise

Think of a time when you thought you were being treated unfairly and answer these questions about the situation:

- Who was involved?
- What assumptions did you make about the other's motives?
- Did you check out your assumptions directly with the other person?
- If you did, were your assumptions true?

Three Basic Needs

To reduce fear and improve relationships we must recognize three basic needs that we all have:

1. We need to be liked.

Our need to be valued and appreciated is a powerful motivator. We instinctively know the value of being liked. Being liked helps us get things done, be promoted, win projects, influence others and gain support. Not being liked leads to conflicts with peers, loss of opportunities, poor cooperation and a bad reputation.

No matter how much we pretend, no one truly *wants* to be disliked. The hardest, toughest people are often the tenderest inside. One manager said to me, "I act like a bear and people are afraid of me, but inside I'm a woos."

Cliques reflect needs

The desire to be liked, feel safe and be appreciated can be seen in cliques. Workplaces are reminiscent of high school when it comes to cliques. We have old-timer cliques, technical cliques, ethnic cliques, smoker cliques, old-boy cliques, manager cliques, front-desk and back-office cliques.

Cliques are normal. They are the natural grouping of people who share an experience or interest in common. Cliques create a sense of belonging, but they also leave people out. It's the simple exclusions such as not being invited to lunch that cause bad feelings. Status symbols such as higher walls, larger offices and reserved parking spaces also create separation. The have-nots feel resentful and envious of the more privileged haves. Employees want to get beyond cliques and superficial differences. They express these feelings as follows: "I wish we could work better together. I want to know more about other groups and departments. I like it when we work as a team."

2. We need to be appreciated.

Appreciating each other can remedy a negative situation. A welfare agency is on the verge of a costly lawsuit with an Asian employee, Wong Lee. Wong Lee is threatening to sue the organization for discrimination. Jim, his manager, is at a loss about what to do. How did the situation get so out of hand? What can he do? To salvage their relationship before the lawyers close in, Jim works with the human resource manager.

After the human resource manager interviews employees, the problem becomes clear. Wong Lee is Asian-American. Jim has little experience managing a culturally diverse group. He sticks with what's comfortable and familiar to him. Unconsciously he gives all his friends the promotions and special assignments. After three years of watching this pattern, Wong Lee is discouraged and angry. He wants to grow and be promoted but he sees little hope of getting help from Jim.

Jim feels intimidated and uncertain around Wong Lee. Wong Lee's English is difficult for Jim to understand. He can't relate to Wong Lee's interests or background.

The first step in rebuilding this nearly disastrous situation is for Jim and Wong Lee to spend time together. Repairing their relationship is not an easy process, especially given their differing pasts. But as Jim gradually gets to know Wong Lee, his appreciation for him grows, as does his appreciation for Wong Lee's talents. Wong Lee starts to feel that his ideas and suggestions are valued. They learn to work together and a costly lawsuit is avoided.

3. We need to belong.

We need to feel that we belong in order to contribute our best. Too often we fail miserably at bonding and connecting with each other. Even in meetings where we don't know each other, little time is spent on introductions and finding common ground. Instead, we dive right into the task and ignore the fact that we don't even know the person sitting next to us.

Lack of attention to the need to belong is evident in the way we treat new employees. Some new employees describe their first day on the job this way:

- "They took me to my desk, showed me my phone and that was it. From there on I was on my own."

- "I showed up in the morning and waited in the lobby until 10:00, when someone finally remembered me."
- "They gave me a perfunctory tour and then everyone left for lunch. I stayed behind and answered the phone."
- "The former sales manager arrived at my house and dumped stuff from the back of his car into my trunk and said, 'Good luck'."

These may sound like horror stories, but for too many employees they're all too real.

Some companies do a wonderful job of bringing new employees on board. New hires attend an orientation session. They hear stories about the company's early beginnings and learn about corporate values first-hand from top managers. This orientation into the community creates a wonderful sense of belonging.

The Value of Connecting

The quality of our relationships is directly related to our job performance and satisfaction. *We need to acknowledge the significance of our relationships with each other.*

Imagine that you have an invisible highway that connects you to others at work. With each person you work with you have a different kind of connection. Some of your relationships are terrific. You can talk about anything; you get lots done and communication flows easily back and forth between you. With another person you have a completely different connection. With this person there are lots of bumps in the road, and delays and unexpected stops. The amount of work you can get done when you have a good relationship highway is radically different from when you're traveling on back roads and one-way streets. Our ability to get work done is directly affected by the quality of our connection to others.

Action Exercise

Positive relationships are productive. Reflect on your coworkers and answer these questions:

- What kind of relational highways do I have with the people I work with?
- Are my relational highways in good repair?
- Where do my relationship highways look like two-lane roads or bumpy back alleys?"

Here are some basic facts about our connection to others:

- Our connections with people are like "highways."
- Relational highways exist in all shapes and sizes.
- Broken or weak highways affect our ability to get work done.
- The quality of our relational highways are visible to others.
- Conflict is more likely if our relational highways are not in good repair.
- Ongoing maintenance and barrier removal are necessary to maintain strong relational highways.

Building Strong Relationships

When our relational highways are strong, fear and mistrust are much less likely to occur. When these connections are weak, we are vulnerable to mistrust and misperceptions. Keeping our relations intact heads off fear and builds the capacity to work effectively together. To eliminate the problems caused by fear and to build healthy connections, there are several things we can do.

1. Express our appreciation.

Employees frequently comment, "I always hear when things go wrong but when things go right, it's just expected."

Managers can change this feeling by making a conscious effort to show appreciation. Small forms of recognition mean a lot. Start acknowledging individuals by sending notes of appreciation and expressing verbal thank-yous. Let bosses, peers and employees know that you notice, care and value what they are contributing.

Set up peer-appreciation programs. In one office employees bought a small bear that everyone nicknamed the "appreciation bear." Every month the bear appeared in someone's office with a thank-you note for actions they took that were "above and beyond" the call of duty. The recipient passed the bear on to someone else the following month. A little acknowledgment goes a long way.

2. Get to know employees as individuals.

In a utility company of over three hundred employees, the chief executive, Gary, calls every employee by name. Gary has trouble remembering names, so he takes the company roster home at night and memorizes it. He knows that personal recognition is the key to employee commitment and to the success of his business.

Frequently I ask individuals in my groups to introduce themselves and share one unknown fact about themselves. Participants sometimes resist because they've worked together for years and already know each other. The results are amazing. Everyone shares personal stories and develops a deeper appreciation for one another. Afterward they complete the work task in less time and with more laughter.

Organizations often sponsor events for employees to socialize, celebrate and get to know each other. These events are a good start, but they need to be optimized for the value they can bring. Without direction, employees sit with colleagues they already know and fail to become acquainted with other groups. Deliberate orchestration of social activities is necessary to help others get better acquainted. Workplace bonding cannot be left to happenstance or it will not occur at a meaningful level.

Getting to know each other and expressing appreciation for one another builds a solid foundation for good working relationships. Without this relational baseline, problems and concerns are more likely to affect productivity.

3. Encourage diverse opinions.

When we work together we need to be able to disagree with each other and still maintain the relationship. Use the following statements to encourage different points of view:

When you disagree with your boss, say:

- "I have an opinion about this decision [or project], but I am hesitant to express it. Do you want to hear my views about this situation?"
- "I'd like to feel that there will be no reprisals if I tell you what I think about this issue."

To encourage divergent opinions and less conformance in a group, say:

- "We have talked about the benefits of this idea; now let's talk about the risks and drawbacks we haven't discussed."
- "Who has an opinion that's vastly different from that of the majority in this room? Let's hear your views and see what we can learn that might help us."

To express a different opinion, you can say:

- "I have an opinion that's different from everyone else's; do you want to hear it?"

To solicit candid feedback about a change, say:

- "I'd like your input on how the new program is working. I especially want to know about the problems and what can be improved. Please speak up, even if you think I won't like what you have to say. Your ideas, insights and feedback are important to me." Thank individuals for their response, *especially* when the answer is not what you want to hear.

4. Seek information in a nonthreatening way.

The kinds of questions we ask determine whether we get an honest answer or an evasive reply. Blaming questions can trigger fear. Interest and curiosity invite responses. Questions that begin with the words "Why" and "Who" can be threatening. They imply that someone is to blame for the problem.

Imagine there's a problem and someone asks you these questions. What is your reaction?

"Why" and "Who" questions:

- "Why did this happen?"
- "Who was here yesterday?"
- "Who is working on this project?"
- "Why does this happen every Monday?"
- "Why did you do that?"

Questions that start with "What" and "How" are less threatening and imply that you want to understand, not blame. Observe the difference in your reaction to the following list of questions:

"What" and "How" questions:

- "How did this occur?"
- "What took place yesterday?"
- "How can we improve our work process?"
- "What causes this to happen every Monday?"
- "What happened?"

When the situation is stressful, it's important to wait for complete responses and to ask more than one question. If you're asking questions, wait for a complete response. Allow time for the person to answer the question.

Faith Ralston Ph.D

What we fear most at work is rejection. If we fail to acknowledge the power of fear, it can wreak havoc at work. We can reduce fear by maintaining positive relationships with each other and making it safe to talk openly about concerns. This takes deliberate time and effort, but the rewards are superior performance and better working relationships.

Business Reality #6: Seventy percent of employees are afraid to speak up for fear of negative repercussions.

Success Action: Drive out fear to promote exceptional communication.

Key Learnings

1. At the heart of fear lives our need to be valued and appreciated.

2. We conform in order to be accepted.

3. We dislike people and situations that damage our self-worth.

4. We can reduce fear by building positive relationships with the people at work.

5. Positive relationships require ongoing maintenance and barrier removal.

Chapter 7

Adopt New Leadership Roles To Meet Changing Work Requirements

So much of what we call management consists in making it difficult for people to work.

Peter Drucker

Boss: Do it this way.
Employee: Why?
Boss: Because I said so!

Functional mindsets and "do what I say" attitudes are obsolete. Computer-savvy employees and horizontally structured organizations require different leadership skills than functional silos of the past. Leadership skills must be in sync with changing business requirements. Today's business environment requires leaders to:

- Articulate and foster clear values.
- Focus on outcomes, not activities.
- Persuade and motivate rather than control and inspect.
- Create high-performing teams committed to common goals.
- Acknowledge and address emotional concerns.
- Lead highly productive meetings.

It is the manager's role to articulate and foster clear values.

A significant part of the manager's job is to articulate the values he or she wants employees to develop at work. Clear values set standards for making decisions and working relationships. Without a commitment to the value of high quality, employees wonder whether to meet production quotas or stop substandard products from going out the door. Organizational values help employees know what's important.

Values shape behaviors. An organization without values is like a relationship without expectations. Clear values help managers and employees know what's important, hold each other to a high standard and challenge unacceptable behavior. Here's an example of one company's value statement:

Our Values

- We respect and utilize the talents of individuals.
- We work collaboratively to meet customer needs.
- We act with integrity in every business decision.
- We empower people to take initiative and make decisions.
- We recognize and acknowledge outstanding performance.
- We create trusting relationships with customers and each other.

Specific behaviors and attitudes that support one of these value statements are as follows:

Value statement: We create trusting relationships with customers and each other.

The behaviors and attitudes that support this statement:

- We make customers our number-one priority.
- We clarify what the customer wants early on.
- We resolve differences with customers in a mutually satisfying way.
- We cooperate across departments to deliver quality services to customers on time.

Implementing Values

The values we hold as a leader need to be communicated and understood by every member of our organization. Value statements must be "living documents," not plaques on the wall.

Leaders make sure that every employee knows the values and is encouraged to live the values. Values need to be talked about and reinforced. Managers and employees ask: "How can we implement our values in this situation? We encourage stories about innovative ways that we are implementing our values."

Values Are Not Always Convenient

Actually "living the values" makes them come alive. One company's commitment to stable employment was put to the test many times. On several occasions, they reduced the work week to four days rather than lay people off. Another organization, whose value was simplicity, replaced their oversized personnel manual with a five-page document describing their values and a preface that said, "These are our values—Do what's right!"

Values encourage feedback. We give and receive feedback about attitudes and behaviors that support our values. If we value cooperation and our behaviors are negative and denigrating to others, we expect to hear about it.

Values Don't Guarantee Success

Even when we strive to live the values, sometimes we fail. Roxanne is a manager who is committed to open communication. But due to a pending merger, she had to lay off employees without prior warning. The ones who remained said, "So much for open communication. Roxanne didn't even tell us what was going on. Why should we trust her? When times get tough, communication goes out the window."

Staying true to our values can be difficult. It means evaluating everything we do and admitting our mistakes. Hard times are the acid test of our values. It's one thing to adhere to our values when business is profitable, but it's tougher when the results aren't there. One organization was put to the test around their commitment to community service when financial pressures mounted and they had to make decisions about their next year's contributions.

Values Won't Fit For Everyone

When organizations identify and live their values, it is easier for employees to know if they belong in that organization. Working in an environment that doesn't value what we value is difficult. Individual fit with organizational values is important.

Suzanne is the manager in a marketing department. She values direct, honest communication and hates political intrigue and favoritism. She works in a "make nice" environment where direct, honest communication is rare. For several years she pushes for change and challenges the way decisions are made. But nothing changes. She receives no encouragement or support for her efforts. Her jaw gets tense and her blood pressure rises; she experiences many physical aches and pains. She is working in an environment that is toxic to her. Suzanne has one set of values and the organization has another. She realizes she'll never win the battle she's fighting. She decides to leave the organization. The clearer the values, the quicker we know if the organization is right for us and vice versa.

Comparing Values to Reality

Sometimes written values are in stark contrast with what people experience. If an organization's "real values" were written down, they might look more like these:

- We value profits over people.
- We value quotas over quality.
- Always look out for number one.
- Team performance is not rewarded.
- If your opinion differs from the people in power, keep it to yourself.

When stated values are inconsistent with reality, the values quickly lose their power and credibility. Employees might say to themselves: "Wait a minute—this morning you said quality was important and now you are asking me to ship this defective product!" We do not believe what we hear—we believe what we see and experience.

Honesty is required to implement our values. Once we define our values, we need to assess the current reality and identify the values that are encouraged by the organization. To check out whether your values match up with your ideal values, answer the following questions.

In your present work situation...

1. What behaviors are in conflict with the stated values?

2. What attitudes undermine the stated values?

3. What norms are in conflict with the stated values?

Advocating values that don't match reality is like "whipped cream on top of worms." It looks good, smells good, but just beneath the surface it's rotten. We are appalled. Company values overlaying mistrust and inequities are equally distasteful. Admitting the truth helps us to act differently. We relax when we hear the truth about a situation, even when it's unpleasant.

The first step is to look for broad discrepancies between your stated values and current practices. Then it's important to identify specific behaviors that you can do something about. These are the findings of one management team that completed this exercise.

Our Values Collide With Reality

Here is one group's assessment of their values and areas where they conflict with current reality:

We value effective leadership.
Current reality:

- We have not communicated a clear direction to the organization.
- We do not follow through on the decisions we make.

We value teamwork and cooperation.
Current reality:

- We have no team award or recognition, only individual recognition.
- The value of teamwork is not communicated in our new employee orientation program.
- We don't cooperate outside our functional area.

We value partnering with the customers.
Current reality:

- Our technical experts have poor customer communication skills.
- We wait until there is a problem to initiate any contact with the customer.

We value risk-taking.
Current reality:

- We are afraid to buck the system.
- We don't challenge decisions.

Addressing the Inconsistencies

Managers who define their values and address inconsistencies are way ahead of those who stop after the defining stage. One management team decided to take these actions to come in line with their values: "To better align with our values, we will change our compensation system to reward team performance, encourage more risk-taking in decisions and train technical personnel in customer skills." These changes motivated a stronger commitment to the values by managers and employees.

The number-one job of management is to articulate and promote clear values. Values encourage consistent behaviors and motivate everyone in the organization to commit to high standards and worthwhile goals.

It is the manager's role to focus on outcomes.

Managers need to focus on outcomes instead of on activities. Focusing on outcomes encourages employees to accept responsibility for reaching their goals. One day over lunch a seasoned manager, Joe, described how his management style changed from control to an "outcome" focus. Picking up a cup from the table, he said, "I used to say, 'We need to move this cup from here to here' and then I would pick up the cup and move it. Now I say, 'We need to move this cup from here to here. Tell me, what's the most effective way to do this?' Now we work *together* to reach the outcomes we want and we are finding innovative ways to get things done better and faster."

An outcome focus requires that we *trust each other rather than control*. When we focus on outcomes, we don't tell others how to achieve the outcome. Instead, we agree on what needs to be done and then give employees the freedom to find solutions.

The following mindsets keep us activity-driven rather than outcome-driven:

- If we are not "doing something," nothing is happening.
- We don't have time to plan.
- If we don't do it, it won't get done.
- It's what we *do* that really counts.

Defining Outcomes

The following ideas will help managers and team leaders clarify outcomes before taking action.

- Ask often: "What are we trying to achieve? What is the purpose of this meeting [project, event]? What outcomes do we want?"
- Avoid the tendency to discuss solutions before defining the problem and desired outcomes. Say frequently: "Let's understand the problem first and what we're trying to achieve, before we talk about solutions."
- Appoint someone as a "monitor" to keep the discussion from detouring prematurely into solutions or "how-tos."
- When solutions are proposed, ask: "What are some additional solutions?" Keep exploring the problem.
- When defining the outcome, be specific: "When we have reached our goal, what will the result look like?" For example, if your goal is to create a better work climate, ask: "How will people actually behave when we have a better work climate?"
- Be sure that everyone understands and agrees upon the outcomes defined. For example: "Let's talk about what we actually mean when we say 'higher profit'."
- Use questions that encourage discussion and dialogue about objectives. Replace the question "Do you understand our objectives?" with the question "What questions or comments do you have about our objectives?"

It is the manager's role to persuade and motivate.

In the new work environment, it is increasingly obvious that mandates don't work. Key decisions that satisfy customers are highly dependent on front-line employees to execute. There will never be enough time or money to ensure compliance to mandates. The new leader must have superb influencing skills in order to motivate employees, because most of the time the manager is not there.

The manager's role is to ensure appropriate input into decisions that affect others. This means the decision-making process is lengthy, convoluted and time-consuming. Getting input from others is messy. Formerly isolated departments are now exploding into full-blown community forums where everyone can voice his or her opinion about what the functional area should or shouldn't be doing. This highly interactive process is exciting and useful but not always comfortable for the manager who is used to having ultimate control over a department and decisions.

It is the manager's role to create high-performing teams.

The manager must coordinate specialists who report to other managers. The manager's team may be composed of individuals who have a history of competing with one another, come from diverse disciplines, have opposing views and question the value of working together. Leading diverse groups is very different from leading groups of like-minded individuals who report to one person.

Groups of people who never imagined themselves in the same room together are now meeting to identify solutions. Unions are working with management to save jobs, special interest groups are collaborating to secure funding, agencies are consolidating to save money and competitors are cooperating to serve their customers. Managers have the task of building effective teams of effective partners and coworkers.

Managers are transitioning from the role of:

- Managing a function to Overseeing processes
- Supervising work to Coordinating resources
- Being the expert to Consulting with experts
- Making decisions to Facilitating agreements
- Enforcing regulations to Securing commitment
- Giving the answers to Asking the questions

In short, the new role of the manager is to link, integrate, access, coordinate and synthesize information from specialized areas in order to solve problems and respond to opportunities.

It is the manager's role to acknowledge and address emotional concerns.

Change is volatile. People will react with anger, mistrust, tears and repressed emotions. The manager needs to be able to walk into a room of angry employees, listen to their points of view, acknowledge their feelings and genuinely respond to their concerns—even when the answers are not what they want to hear. Tensions that are avoided do not go away. If a manager can facilitate these situations in a constructive way, the chances of success on a project are much greater.

When I was growing up, my mother used to say, "No news is good news." Too many managers have this communication philosophy as well. The belief is: We don't want to upset people or deal with unnecessary speculation. If employees were unaware of what was happening, this might be a possibility, but they *are* aware. Managers must learn to talk about difficult issues before they are decided and give employees time to discuss and understand the implications. This means no more one-way communication meetings. Involving employees in changes and decisions must be done early and often. Employee guessing and speculation squander too much time and energy. If leaders tap this energy they can use it to promote loyalty, solicit implementation ideas and gain commitment to changes early in the process.

It is the manager's role to lead highly productive meetings.

Managers can spend up to ninety percent of their time in meetings. Meetings are the most precious use of time that an organization has. Every person present represents time and money that needs to be honored by the way a meeting is run. Most managers dread meetings. Too much time is spent listening to the dominant person's point of view, discussing issues with no follow-through, talking about details that are not important and reporting on projects with no meaningful discussion. Meetings are often highly ritualized events—designed to keep anything that is controversial from coming to the surface.

Meetings need to become places where the real issues are discussed, creative options are explored, agreements are reached, decisions are made and actions are decided. Much help is available to improve meeting effectiveness. Simple changes can bring immediate improvement:

- Set an agenda.
- Start the meeting on time.
- Allow time for discussion.
- Clarify the format.
- Rotate the leadership.
- Record important decisions.

Make sure that individuals know the role you want them to play at different times in the meeting. Specify whether you want them to:

1. Generate new ideas.
2. Listen and understand.
3. Make a decision.
4. Critique and give feedback.

Another simple yet highly effective process that can be used to improve meeting and group effectiveness is a plus-and-minus chart. At the end of a meeting, group members write their responses to three questions on a flipchart:

1. In this meeting, I liked (+) the following: (procedures, behaviors, attitudes, beliefs, achievements).
2. In this meeting, I disliked (-) the following: (procedures, behaviors, attitudes, beliefs, achievements).

3. In our next meeting, we want to make the following changes: (procedures, behaviors, attitudes, beliefs, achievements).

Much help is available to improve meeting effectiveness. Managers can use video feedback, engage a process consultant, take time to self-critique and even use computerized decision-making technology to improve meeting effectiveness. We need to become intolerant of ineffective meetings, realize the opportunity present and resist the norm that says, "We've always done it this way."

The Need for Facilitation Skills

To meet these challenges, the modern manager needs the skills of facilitation as much as the shoemaker of old needed a hammer. It is virtually impossible to address opposing points of view, encourage differences of opinions, handle emotional reactions, create synergy among separate individuals, discuss issues that affect job security, build a team out of strangers and gain commitment to decisions—without the skills of facilitation. The ability to facilitate is a fundamental underpinning for modern management. Most managers are not trained in facilitation skills and using them feels strange and awkward at first.

Use of problem-solving skills alone leads to sterile analysis and neglect of interpersonal issues that affect teamwork and trust; whereas using facilitation skills alone produces a warm sense of bonding but fails to provide adequate analysis, understanding and solution of the issues.

Implications for Managers

New attitudes, skills and behaviors are required for the manager to step into this new role. The manager must be a master at dealing with people, understanding interpersonal dynamics and needs, gaining commitment, ensuring participation, leading groups, facilitating discussion and resolving differences of opinion. To move into this role, the manager must frequently let go of outdated beliefs and attitudes such as the following:

"I must know everything."

A manager becomes extremely nervous when his boss called and asked for the details of a report. He frets, "When my boss calls about a project, he expects me to have the answer immediately. I'd better know or be able to find out within the hour. But it's virtually impossible to let people make their own decisions and still know everything that's going on. Expecting managers to know all the details keeps us focused on a level of detail that's not beneficial to the organization.

"It's not my problem."

The manager must assume responsibility for problems outside their sphere of control. Zed, the new product manager, takes credit when sales volume is up, but he also needs to feel equally responsible when the customer service department is swamped with complaints about the product. We must take ownership of the whole, not just our part.

"I want immediate results."

The issues we face will not be solved overnight. Lasting solutions can require months to implement. Too quickly, we become impatient with the laborious work of teams and involvement processes. The desire for immediate results affects the way we spend our time. We are attracted to firefighting and handling operational issues because we can see tangible results. But we must loosen our grip on quick fixes or we will still be handling today's problems tomorrow.

To be effective in their new role, a manager must be able to create climates where it's safe to tell the truth, address emotional concerns of oneself and others, and lead highly productive meetings.

The Magnitude of The Change

We underestimate what is required to make even modest changes in our management style. Changing our expectations and assumptions about the manager's role is a revolution, not an evolution, of what we do today. Old habits die hard and some of them are necessary. The manager is betwixt and between in the transition to a new management style.

The greatest amount of support for change in the manager's role is needed at the top. Changes in management style made at the executive level will permeate the organization; whereas individual style changes tend to remain in isolated pockets. A fundamental truth in organizations is: *We tend to manage as we are managed.*

We can no longer expect managers to treat employees in ways that they, themselves, are not treated. Nor can we expect managers to change simply because they are paid well. Money from a paycheck cannot replace the need for support. We do not outgrow our need for practice, encouragement and support when making a significant change.

We would like to believe that we are capable of swallowing this elephant in one bite, but this is not possible. We may want to go to one major event and have it change us forever. But overcoming decades of traditional management behaviors will take time. Behavioral change requires bite-sized bits of knowledge and skill practice over time to become a way of life. Anything less is simply motivational training, or awareness training, and will fall away within weeks. Successful programs designed to help individuals achieve significant change—such as Weight Watchers, Alcoholics Anonymous, athletic training, language schools and music lessons—require consistent practice, support and application over an extended period of time. *There is no quick fix.*

A Worthy Investment

Managers need to engage in regular, ongoing sessions of skill development and discussions about how management skills can be applied to routine work activity. Management teams need to become virtual support groups for transforming assumptions and behaviors—places where new skills are learned, information is shared, assumptions are challenged, concerns are expressed and experiences are shared. Managers can learn from each other's successes and failures.

One hour a week or two hours every other week is a minimal investment necessary to transform management skills. Commitment to a year of learning is a realistic expectation for change to occur. We readily make this type of commitment to new software programs and production technology. Now it is time to make this type of commitment to leadership development. Skilled managers who provide leadership for the future are the most valuable asset organizations have.

Business Reality #7: Current work requires radically different behaviors than imprints from the past.

Success Action: Adopt new leadership roles to meet changing work requirements.

Key Learnings

1. Clearly articulated values tell employees what's expected.

2. The discrepancies between our values and real-life practices need to be reconciled.

3. Values promote consistent standards for everyone in the organization.

4. The new role of leaders is to:

   - Articulate and foster clear values.
   - Focus on outcomes, not on activities.
   - Persuade and motivate rather than control and inspect.
   - Create high-performing teams committed to common goals.
   - Acknowledge and address emotional concerns.
   - Lead highly productive meetings.

Chapter 8

Develop Mutual Respect To Strengthen Supervisory Relationships

If you can't get rid of the family skeleton, you may as well make it dance.

George Bernard Shaw

My son writes to me from abroad: "Dear Mom, I got a job in a factory. I even got promoted to manager. This means that if there are problems in my area, it's *my* fault instead of my boss!"

Recent surveys indicate that the vast majority of employees who quit their job are actually quitting their *manager*! Fifty percent of employees say the relationship with their boss is "suboptimal." And the reason most cited for not wanting to go to work in the morning is *the boss*!

Confusion About New Roles

Radical changes in our roles are making these relationships tenuous. Hierarchical behaviors are no longer appropriate but new behaviors are not well established. We dance around each other, unsure of what to expect. One minute employees hear "You're empowered" and the next minute they hear "Do what you're told." Managers complain about employee passivity and employees wish their managers would get out of the way. Silently, managers wonder:

- Am I giving up too much control?
- Will employees be accountable?
- Should I intervene?
- Can I trust them to do this?

Silently, employees wonder:

- Is my boss happy with what I'm doing?
- What does my manager expect?
- How much autonomy do I really have?

We hesitate to break with tradition, yet we can't move ahead without doing so. Under these conditions misunderstanding and conflicts are bound to arise.

In the past there simply weren't as many opportunities for manager/employee relationships to conflict. And if they did, we knew who was going to win. In our new roles, the key questions are:

- How do we resolve our differences?
- How do we address missed expectations, disagreements and authority issues?

All we can imagine is reverting to the past, which is no longer appropriate or effective. We have lost our underpinnings.

Unraveling the Issues

Before we can adopt more effective roles, we must see the underlying dynamics and assumptions that keep traditional practices alive. Beneath the surface we find family dynamics being played out in organizational life. Referencing family roles helps us understand our unconscious expectations in manager/employee roles. The archetypal roles of mom, dad, parent and child set the stage for roles in hierarchical business relationships.

Let's consider the basic assumptions we have about family roles. The parents are expected to help the child grow so that one day he or she can become a responsible adult. We believe that parents should be respected and children should be treated fairly. We discourage favoritism among the kids. We realize that when the parents fight, children get caught in the middle. We recognize that it's good for parents to have time for themselves.

We know that abusive, permissive and overcontrolling parents don't create healthful environments for their children. We notice that some individuals are better at parenting than others are.

At work managers unconsciously step into the role of parents, the ones who are expected to "do what's right, take care of the kids and make responsible decisions." And employees unconsciously step into the role of children, the ones who "need protection, nurturing and development and are expected to be obedient." In the corporate world, there are both "mom" and "dad" roles: "moms" are the caregivers; "dads" are the decision-makers. A man or woman can play either role. For example, Wanda, the director of the information technology department, is in the child's role with her boss; she plays the "dad" role with her employees. Behaviors and authority levels determine unconscious role expectations.

Expectations and Assumptions

Now replace the word "parents" with the word "managers." Managers are responsible for caring for employees and directing work activity. Employees are responsible for learning, producing and getting along with their peers. Employees want to please their managers. Approval means a lot. Employees are experts at reading the cues, anticipating their manager's needs and sensing favoritism and disapproval. Unspoken role expectations lead to disappointment and frustration. Managers and employees are disappointed when others fail to live up to their expectations.

Importance of Relationships at the Top

Just as the relationship between "mom and dad" affects the kids, the relationships among primary leaders affect the level of cooperation and cohesion among employees. Will, the president of a bank, prefers to work on external issues and expects Brian, his operations manager, to run the day-to-day business.

However, Brian and Will do not respect each other's abilities. Each sees the other as deficient in some way.

To deal with their differences, they agree to stay out of each other's territory. They're like a married couple who share the same house but sleep in separate bedrooms. Brian and Will's solution solves their interpersonal problems but the bank's operation suffers. Will's new ideas and customer perspectives don't get incorporated into the business. In the short term the bank is highly profitable, but over time it fails to adapt to the changing marketplace. At the heart of the problem is the breakdown between the president and the operations manager. Basically, the "parents" don't communicate and the entire family suffers.

Employees Act Out

When leaders don't cooperate, employees get mixed messages and feel emotionally pulled to "take sides."

Jack, a strong-willed employee, ignores his supervisor, Sally, and goes directly to the department manager, Lee, to ask for direction and advice. Jack complains to Lee about Sally's incompetence as a manager. Silently Lee agrees with Jack's comments, but he never talks to Sally. Lee gives Jack a sympathetic ear and then tells Sally to "handle Jack's problem." Lee doesn't realize that he's undermining Sally as a manager and making things worse.

The situation is resolved when Lee talks directly to Sally about his expectations and they agree on ways to improve their communication. By improving their relationship, Sally and Lee create a better working situation for Jack.

When employees aren't getting along, always look up and see if there's tension among the next-level managers. Conflicts may be subtle, but employees act them out. Often, the best solution to employee conflicts is to resolve issues among their managers and then employee tensions magically disappear.

Sibling Rivalry

Just as brothers and sisters fight and compete with each other, so do employees, often to get the attention of their superiors. A standard practice in many companies is for the CEO to set up competition among his staff to see who will replace him or her. In some circles this practice is considered good management, when in reality it breaks down the cooperation that's essential to leading the organization.

Internal competition suboptimizes performance. Managers and employees compete for higher positions, more status, larger budgets, better bonuses and greater power and control. Competition leads to withholding information, undermining, backbiting and lack of cooperation. In highly competitive environments, people work for their own advancement and not for the good of the organization and its customers. Internal rivalry needs to be stopped because it siphons enormous amounts of energy from battling the real competitors.

Inept Managers

Just as there are adults who should not be parents, there are individuals who should not manage people. There are three types of management behaviors that create problems for employees and the organization:

- Abusive behaviors
- Permissive behaviors
- Controlling behaviors

Abusive behaviors

Much like abusive parents, abusive managers use their power in ways that are emotionally damaging to employees' well-being.

One such manager, Bill, is well-known in the company for his abusive treatment of employees. Bill is a high-level vice president in an electrical company. When someone makes a "mistake," Bill calls the person into his office and verbally abuses him or her. He rants, yells and shames the person. His tirades can last from thirty minutes to over two hours, depending on how long it takes the employee to break down. Everyone knows when these meetings are happening. But no one steps in or questions Bill's abusive behavior. The silent rule is "Never interfere in the relationship between a boss and employee."

The human resource manager may discuss the problem with Bill, but he or she is powerless to take action unless Bill's superior is supportive of change. As long as Bill and others like him hit their numbers, top management stays out of the way. Abusive behaviors happen every day and are silently condoned.

At work emotional abuse is as devastating as physical abuse. Angry, insecure managers intimidate people who dare not fight back. Someone needs to intervene. Abusive behavior will not stop unless clear messages are sent that this behavior is unacceptable and will result in termination if continued.

Permissive behaviors

Permissive managers do as much if not more damage than abusive managers do. Permissive managers let the ship steer itself. They're afraid to take the helm and ultimately frustrate everyone who reports to them.

Wynel is appointed commissioner at a state agency. She does not like conflict or disagreement. When employees come to Wynel with their ideas, she approves them all. If a project receives heavy public criticism, she lets her staff hang out to dry. In Wynel's department decisions are left to chance, personnel issues are ignored and projects stall from lack of leadership and support.

The ability to take a stand, make decisions and address conflicts is central to the role of a manager. Passive managers need to meet the challenges of leading or let someone else take over.

Controlling behaviors

Just as there are parents who try to control their children and keep them from making mistakes, there are managers who tightly control their people and keep them from growing.

Gary manages an administrative department for an insurance company. His people are extremely unhappy. They say, "Gary treats us like babies. We've been doing this work for five years and we still have to go to him for every decision. We feel like idiots waiting for him to tell us what to do."

Gary is an overly controlling manager. Employee unrest is shouting at Gary to let go and develop his employees. Gary's talents and interests reside in his technical expertise, not in managing people.

Overcontrolling managers keep employees from learning and growing from their mistakes.

Status as Manager

Not all individuals want to manage people. Yet it's difficult to gain status without becoming a manager. As one manager put it, "If you're not a manager, you're not a serious player." The current value we place on being a manager is so highly institutionalized that it will take extraordinary measures to release ourselves from this mindset. Our priorities are in the wrong place. We need to make "management" a specialized position that is not the *only* way to make money and feel important.

The best managers develop their people. Employees talk about Jerry, who's an excellent manager. "Jerry has a way of inspiring us to do great things. We know he cares about us. We'll go the extra mile for him." People always remember how it feels to be managed by someone who believes in them.

New Role of Management

The role of managers is to help employees grow up. Specifically, managers need to:

- Encourage responsibility and accountability for results.
- Create environments of cooperation and teamwork.
- Help employees learn from their mistakes.
- Set standards and hold people accountable.

A good manager helps employees accept responsibility and responds to their requests for help. She or he spends time talking to employees and getting to know the issues they face. When employees come to managers for help, they understand the situation and solve the problem together. They build a team and encourage individuals to rely upon each other. When employee tensions arise, they encourage them to speak directly to each other and work things out. Good managers also facilitate conflict resolution when necessary.

New Role for Employees

The employee's role also changes. When children grow up, sometimes they don't want to leave home. Growing up is both wonderful and frightening. When the mother bird nudges the babies out of the nest, it's the babies who have to fly. Flying can be terrifying.

Some employees don't want to change. New behaviors are risky to initiate. Not everyone is ready at the same time. Many watch as the first ones step over the edge. They watch to see if the ones who take off get supported and survive. If it looks safe, they might try. What happens to the early risk-takers is critical. If they get beat up, punished, fired, displaced or criticized by management, no one will follow their lead. And why should they?

As managers open the door to decision-making and greater responsibility, employees need to walk through the door. The act of walking through this door needs to be respected because it means accepting responsibility. Responsibility fundamentally changes the nature of the employee's relationship to his or her manager. It's graduation day. The supervisor is no longer to blame. All the things we always wanted to try become possibilities to explore; the rules others enforced must be examined to see if they make sense. "Us versus them" is a game of the past. Instead of blaming management, we seek information and support. When we need something, we ask for it. When we see something wrong, we talk about it. When we want something to be different, we take action.

We don't do it alone. We realize that managers have information and perspectives that we need. We understand that our actions have implications for others and we get approval before blazing ahead. Blind obedience is replaced with curiosity; compliance is replaced with initiative. Becoming responsible means looking our old job in the face and seeing all the ways it could be better. We know what needs to get done and we take responsibility for doing it.

Our current work relationships may be far from this vision. The change will not happen overnight. It takes consistent actions over time to change old patterns of behavior.

Addressing Our Differences

In the meantime, how do we address the issues and differences that come up? When manager/employee relationships break down, how do we resolve our differences in a new way? Troublesome situations are the new classrooms that can help us develop the skills we're missing. Conflicts provide opportunities to move into new roles and more productive relationships.

Step 1: Seek level ground.

The first step in resolving workplace differences is to seek level ground. We go nowhere when we stay in one-up, one-down positions. To build a better relationship we must start on equal footing. This means communicating to the employee: "Your needs are as important as my needs. I'm interested in your point of view and I want you to hear mine."

The most common question that employees have at this point is, "If I open up and share my opinions and feelings, is it safe?" This is a valid question and deserves an honest response before the dialogue begins.

Create equal footing by meeting in a neutral location, not your office or theirs.

Set ground rules for the conversation, such as:

- It is safe to be candid.
- We will be respectful.
- We will listen and understand each other's point of view.

Describe the incident/behavior that concerns you. Listen to the other's point of view. Summarize their point of view and acknowledge it. Do not try to solve the problem at this time.

During the conversation take turns. Each person takes fifteen to thirty minutes for his or her turn. Before the second person shares, the first person summarizes what they heard. Avoid simultaneous talking or debating of what's said.

When it's your turn, share how you feel and what you want to be different. You might say: "It bothered me when you did this..." "I don't like it when..." "What I really want is..." and so forth until both sides have shared and heard each other.

As we talk and listen, we need to acknowledge and forgive each other's humanness. We make mistakes and we hurt each other. Just as our parents did not mean to hurt us, or our children do not mean to ignore us, neither do we deliberately hurt one another. Our mistakes are born out of our humanness. What helps is to understand how we hurt each other. After we've understood the hurts, we need to move on. Trying to suppress our feelings doesn't work. We must let go and move on.

Step 2: Focus on the task.

The next phase of the process is to look at our shared responsibilities and make decisions about what we need to do together. Focusing on shared goals is healing and creates a sense of purpose. Discuss and agree on what you need to accomplish together. Consider:

- What is the situation in front of us?
- What needs to be done?
- Where do we need to work together?

Reach agreement on what you need to do together and move on to step three and talk about how you're going to work with each other in a new way.

Step 3: "Make it up."

The final step in the process is to decide how you will work together. This step is called "Make it up" because there are no longer any rules such as "You are the boss, so tell me what to do." In this step you have the opportunity to shed former roles and expectations and make new agreements about how you'll work together based on your desires and preferences. The ways you choose to interact are based on your mutual needs, rather than on any prescribed set of rules.

- Discuss and agree on the roles you want to have in the project or work.
- Make decisions about behaviors and expectations of each other.
- Agree to the specific time period where you will "try out" new behaviors.
- Set a time to follow up and discuss what's working and what's not working.

In this step it's important to make your agreements simple and easy to implement. Give yourselves time to try out new behaviors and discover what works. Stay connected and talk about how things are working between you. Refine and modify as you go, rather than trying to change everything at once.

Relating As Adults

Traditional roles are fading as new structures and work requirements demand new roles. We are moving into adult relationships with each other where teamwork and mutual respect replace authority and compliance to rules. What we feel when our kids grow up and are successful is nostalgia and an enormous amount of pride. The same feelings happen in our boss/employee relationships. As we learn to collaborate in new ways, the feeling we have is pride—pride in who we are becoming, pride in watching the other grow and pride in what we can accomplish together.

Business Reality #8: The majority of employees who quit their job are actually quitting their manager.

Success Action: Develop mutual respect to strengthen supervisory relationships.

Key Learnings

1. Radical changes in manager/employee roles are making these relationships tenuous.

2. Employees act out when there's conflict at the next level up in the management structure.

3. Like brothers and sisters, employees compete to get the attention of their superiors.

4. Internal rivalry takes enormous energy away from beating real competitors.

5. The role of the manager is to help employees grow.

6. It takes courage for employees to accept responsibility.

7. We need to acknowledge and forgive each other's humanness to resolve our differences.

Chapter 9

Leverage Individual Talents To Deliver Higher Value

The best retention policies are employees who are excited to come to work.

Author unknown

As organizations respond to a highly competitive marketplace, job change and insecurity become a way of life. Managers lay off employees, displace work overseas, hire outside contractors, buy and sell companies, reorganize departments, assign individuals to new positions and require different skills for current jobs. Employment uncertainty has never been so high. Some of us remember when going to work for an organization was considered a "lifetime commitment" and the standard expectation was internal promotion, longevity of tenure and guaranteed employment.

There is no place in the organization where the uncertainties of change are not affecting people. Executives feel as insecure about their positions as do front-line employees. Many come to work every day and wonder: Will I have a job for the rest of the year? Will I be moved to a new location? When will my manager or job assignment change? How will the new computer system, reorganization, strategy or organizational initiative affect my job? Externally, we are busy with work tasks; internally, we are pondering what will happen next and how it will affect us.

New Career Opportunities

For some, the rapid changes have created unforeseen opportunities as the need for new products and services accelerates.

- Jeanne, a sales consultant, has expanded her business into services for accountants, engineers and lawyers who realize they must market and sell their services, not just respond to phone calls.
- Don, who holds a repetitive production job, has developed the skills to be a team leader and now trains employees in factory locations across the country.
- Brenda, a talented administrative assistant, started learning about computers ten years ago. Today she is overseeing the installation of a new computer system for the entire company. Her career has grown in ways she never thought possible as an administrative assistant.

Career Dilemmas

Risk and opportunity go hand in hand. The following are career dilemmas that individuals find themselves facing in the rapidly changing job market.

- *Desire to create something new.* Matt is a business developer who enjoys starting new companies. As soon as the business or venture is successful, Matt wants to start another new company. But now he's stuck managing one of his companies. He longs for a job that involves more risk.
- *Burned out but afraid to leave.* Will, a senior finance manager, is frustrated. He thinks: There must be more to life than this! I'd like to teach and live on a horse ranch—perhaps do something with my hands. I'm tired of working just to pay the bills. I'm realizing that this is my life.
- *Current work demands restrict upward mobility.* Betty wants to move into marketing but heavy work demands require that she stay in her current position. She considers moving to a new company to achieve her goals.

A great deal of work effectiveness is lost when we are in positions that are not suited to our interests and priorities. It is difficult to imagine how much productivity would be achieved if our talents were matched precisely with our interests and abilities.

I remember when I lost my desire to work. It was distressing because not only did I need to feed my family, I had to get them through college! Over a period of six months my desire to work completely left me. I drove to my office with tears streaming down my face because I didn't want to go there. I couldn't believe I didn't want to work anymore. I did not want to facilitate a group, listen to skeptical employees or help managers plan a change process. I thought to myself, "What is the point? Nothing is going to change. I am wasting their time and mine." I lost hope that anything in the corporate world would ever change. Yes, in the past I had glimmers of hope that a change might take place. Then I remembered how often someone pulled the plug, or the organization changed direction or lost interest in the project. Overall, the end result was too much activity and too little significant change. I felt like the Pied Piper who led employees down the primrose path to no avail. (This is a hard place for a change consultant to be.) This was my work and I did not believe in it anymore. Work had lost its meaning.

During this time a fellow consultant said to me, "Faith, you must engage with your work at a deeper level." At the time, I didn't have a clue what she meant. It took several months of wandering before her statement took on real meaning. Gradually I began to see that my new work was to *face* the resistance I saw, to talk and write about it and to help people address barriers to change in themselves. The process of finding a deeper purpose was full of waiting, anxiety, financial stress, self-doubt, disinterest in work, extreme highs and lows and anything but comfort. The changes taking place inside of me were overwhelming and disconcerting. I simply could not go forward without addressing my concerns.

Our emotions tell us when there is a change in the wind. Feelings of boredom, frequent illness, shortened tempers, lack of energy, repeated failure and even grief tell us we need to make a change. At work our activities may increase or decrease, but either way we won't feel the same sense of satisfaction we once did. What used to work for us doesn't work anymore. When these signs occur, there are new doors and interests that are trying to get our attention. If we listen to our feelings, internal nudging and emerging interests, they will lead us to new possibilities and work situations that are better suited for us. Listening to our feelings helps us turn our attention toward what excites us and brings us joy and renewed energy. The cure for burnout is not rest, but to engage with work at a deeper level.

The Opportunity

To take advantage of more fluid work environments, we must break from habitual attitudes and behaviors that limit the support we offer for career exploration and change. Aligning individual talents with organizational needs requires that we make it safe for individuals to explore career interests. Specifically, we need to:

Encourage employees to get into the right job

We need to stop rejecting people when they don't fit into our organization and help them find a place to contribute. Denise was employed in a small firm as a marketing assistant, but her skills were not in this area. Denise's manager was constantly frustrated because the numbers she calculated were wrong and the reports she prepared were incomplete.

An opportunity for Denise to apply her talents happened when the company decided to move to a new location. Denise was put in charge of the move. Immediately, she started to excel. She oversaw every detail, made hundreds of arrangements, planned and organized schedules with precision and successfully orchestrated every detail of the move. Thanks to her efforts, the scheduled move went like clockwork.

Once the move was over, Denise returned to the marketing job and her poor performance returned with her. Her manager did not know what to do. Denise had just provided a tremendous service to the company, but now the organization no longer needed her skills. After numerous, unsuccessful attempts at coaching Denise to do her current job, the manager fired her. Denise was devastated and left the office in a huff.

In the traditional mindset, it was assumed that Denise would adapt herself to the work of the company or find a new job that met her interests. But Denise needed more help than this. From her manager, she needed (a) specific information about what she was good at doing, (b) clear direction that she must look for this type of work in another company, and (c) encouragement, support and strategies to find a job that matched her interests and skills.

Typically, managers have not considered it their responsibility to provide this much support to an employee, especially if the person is going to work for another organization.

Give and seek feedback

To help employees use their talents and get into the right jobs, we need to give and receive abundant feedback. Managers say that giving performance feedback is the most difficult part of their job. Some avoid giving feedback altogether.

One such manager, Alice, spent two years supervising Beth, an employee she did not believe was capable of doing her job. Rather than discuss this issue with Beth, Alice avoided her, didn't consider her for special projects and silently judged her work as unprofessional. Privately, she wished Beth would find another job. Beth knew something was wrong but could not identify the problem. Lack of feedback created an insidious environment of mistrust.

Receiving feedback is extremely beneficial. It helps us know how we are being perceived by others. Sometimes we are surprised by the feedback; other times we disagree; but overall we benefit by knowing how others see us. Too frequently we dance around the issues we have with each other. We say "That went fine" when we need to say "Your style is overbearing and kept others from participating" or "The presentation did not go well because you included too many details." Giving someone feedback is a *caring activity.* It means that we are willing to take the time to help them improve by talking about their strengths and weaknesses.

All individuals need feedback. The higher up we go in the organization, the more people there are that are influenced by our behavior. Not all employees want to receive feedback on their performance. Managers are fearful of emotional reactions from employees who might not like their comments. Success with performance feedback requires more from us than compliance to annual performance reviews or the use of sophisticated forms. *It requires that we have a relationship with each other that is built on trust.* The person receiving the feedback must know that we are on their side. Within the context of a supportive relationship, positive and negative feedback are very useful. Without this type of relationship, suggestions for improvement can generate feelings of inadequacy and shame.

Provide Support for Exploration

To optimize talents we should allow employees to explore new areas where they have no previous experience. Megan was a successful manager of human resources but she wanted to try her hand at something completely different. She applied for a job as manager of distribution in the marketing department.

For the first nine months Megan struggled to learn the technology and the products. After an intense learning curve on technical issues, Megan created an entirely new distribution system. Megan was successful because she possessed excellent strategic thinking, communication skills and the ability to learn the technical aspects of the job. Too often, however, we won't allow people to stretch this far from what they have done in the past.

To support career exploration, encourage employees to conduct informational interviews and learn about different jobs. Create job exchange programs where employees can work in other areas on special assignments. Provide assessment and testing services to help employees define their skills and abilities. Help employees discover their talents and where their talent can be fully engaged.

The Talent Opportunity

Imagine how much more effective we would be if our talents precisely matched our jobs and work requirements. Work is meant to be a beautiful expression of who we are and what we can contribute to the world. The time is ripe to focus on what we can contribute. The closer we come to using our talents, the more we can contribute.

Each of us has unique talents. Talents are what we do easily and naturally. When we're using our talents we feel satisfied and fulfilled, not drained or depleted. Talents are our doorways to success. When we're doing what we do best, we're unstoppable! Teams who value each other's talents complete projects early. Organizations that recognize individuals' talents are filled with motivated employees. Managers who help employees use their talents achieve excellent business results.

Career Versus Talent

Focusing on our talents is fundamentally different from focusing on our careers. Careers are about what we learn to do; talents are about what we do naturally. A career requires us to get a degree and learn skills to be a doctor, educator, engineer or computer technician. To develop our careers we look for opportunities that fit our training, skills and background. On the job we take on specific responsibilities, tasks and duties. We learn what's expected of us and we do it. If we're successful we're given more responsibility. Typically the better we manage our responsibilities, the more people, budget, resources and visibility we receive.

Talents are innate. We don't have to learn them. They're already a part of us. When we look for our talent, we search for what we do naturally. We ask questions such as: "What's at the heart of everything I do?" "What do I bring that's of value to others regardless of the job I'm in?" When we're offering our talents, we feel joyful. The more we contribute our talents, the more joy we feel.

Career	**Talent**
• Learned skills	• Natural abilities
• Job assignments	• Contribution
• More responsibility	• More joy

Ideally our career and talents go hand in hand. The more we use our natural talents at work, the more satisfaction we experience in our careers.

Knowing our talent sets us up for success. We stop trying to be all things to all people and start focusing on what we do best. We know what we're good at and we let others know what we can contribute. Work becomes easy, fulfilling and highly productive.

Talents Are Natural

Our talents show up everywhere we go—at home, at work and in leisure activities. If our talent is organizing, we organize our desk, projects and closets—and other people, if they let us. If our talent is planning, we plan vacations, block parties, school picnics and projects at work. If we're good problem-solvers, we uncover countless issues to resolve, both at home and at work.

Our natural talents are easy for us. We mistakenly assume that everyone else has the same ability. An innovative systems analyst feels annoyed when coworkers are "blind" to creative solutions. A meticulous planner is frustrated when others overlook obvious problems. A visionary leader feels alone because s/he's the only one who sees what's coming in the future. We expect others to possess the same talent that we do and we feel surprised and disappointed when they don't. We fail to recognize the uniqueness of our own natural talents.

To define our talent we start by asking: "What am I already good at doing? What is so much a part of my nature that I can't stop doing it?" Once we define our talent we ask, "Where can I use my talent and make a real contribution? What job or career lets me fully use these gifts?" Knowing our talent helps us find jobs and careers that suit us.

Finding Our talent

There are three essential steps to finding and using your talent:

1. **See it:** Recognize your unique gift.

2. **Name it:** Clearly articulate your talent.

3. **Do it:** Develop what you do best.

The first step is to identify our unique talents. Next, we name our talents succinctly and let others know what we have to offer. Finally, we develop our talents by finding more and more ways to use them.

1. See It

For most of us, our talents are invisible. They come naturally to us. We don't recognize our talent as unique gifts. We think: Of course I organize my calendar for the entire year—doesn't everybody do that? or Of course I think of ninety-nine possible solutions to every problem—doesn't everybody do this? We are often *blind* to our own talents.

We must first recognize our talents before we can take full advantage of them. To identify your talents, answer these five questions:

1. What are my favorite projects or activities? At work? At home? In social situations? *This question helps you identify where you're already using your talent. Remember, your talent shows up everywhere you do.* Do

you like to clean up messes and organize things? Are you the one everyone turns to talk to about his or her problems? Do you enjoy organizing the Sunday school program and Girl Scouts weekend retreats? Are you a do-it-yourself person who loves to work with your hands? Whatever you like to do and do often, provide valuable clues to your core talents.

2. What do you do even when no one is paying you to do it? At home? At work? *This question helps you identify the activities you gravitate toward.* Look outside of the work setting to discover your talents. When do you feel enthusiastic about an activity or event? What do you naturally want to do when no one is asking you to do anything?

3. What do others consistently ask you to do? *This question helps you see how others are already using your talents.* What do your friends and coworkers want from you? When do they call you and for what? What do you enjoy doing with friends and colleagues? What do others receive from you as a friend?

4. When do you lose interest and enthusiasm for an activity or project? *This question helps you see when your talent is no longer required and may even be getting in the way.* When do you get bored with a project? When do you want to delegate work to someone else? When do you first get interested in a job or project? When do you lose interest? At the beginning? In the middle? At the end of the project? Notice when your energy goes up and when it goes flat. The level of enthusiasm you have for what you're doing is a clue as to where your talents lie.

5. When do others get annoyed with you? This question is often the best clue of your talent. Our greatest strength is also our greatest weakness. We overuse our talents, especially when we don't know what our talents are. Unrecognized talents are dangerous. We rely on our

talent even when it's not needed. For instance, a skillful planner ignores creative input because she's too logical. A take-charge manager unwittingly discourages others from sharing their ideas. A research scientist continues to gather data long after it's time for a solution. An entrepreneur takes unnecessary risks when it's critical to play it safe. There's an old saying: "To someone with a hammer everything looks like a nail." When we know our talents, we can optimize our strengths and minimize our weaknesses.

2. Name It

Naming your talents helps you value your talents. Name yours by condensing what you do well into one simple statement that you can easily communicate to others.

Action Exercise

Read the following instructions and write a Talent Statement in the three parts described below. Start with just one of your talents and do the rest later.

I am a/an ____

____

(Write **adjectives** that describe the unique qualities you bring to every situation: *innovative, creative, clearheaded, easygoing, determined, sensible, accurate, inspiring,* etc.) After listing quite a few, select (circle) the one that fits you best. Get help on this from those who know you well.

____

____

(Write **nouns** that describe the roles you are likely to play: *leader, analyzer, problem-solver, coach, planner, organizer, inventor, motivator,* etc.) Again, list more than one and then narrow it down to the one that fits you best.

***...who helps others* ______________________________**
____.
(Describe **the benefits** others get from your talent: *resolve problems, discover new ideas, move off the dime, launch projects, integrate ideas,* etc.*)* Look for bottom-line benefits (such as *save time, take action, make it easier to...,* etc.).

Remember to keep your Talent Statement simple. Here are few examples:

- I am a creative problem-solver who helps others implement their ideas.
- I am a pioneering researcher who helps others find practical solutions.
- I am an inspirational coach who helps others launch new endeavors.

Action Exercise

Below is a list of fifteen possible talents. Identify several talents that are easy for you:

Creator
I love to create something new. I take abstract ideas and turn them into concrete projects (or products or services) that others can use. However, once the idea or project is flushed out, I lose interest.

Implementer
I am an action-oriented person. I know how to get things done. I often don't come up with the original idea, but I know how to make things happen. Just tell me what's needed and turn me loose. Everything starts moving when I'm involved.

Facilitator

I like to keep the process moving. I make sure that people are getting along and focusing on what needs to be done. I see the value of different views and help people appreciate other perspectives.

Visionary

I see where we need to go in the future. My ideas are ahead of their time. I can imagine what does not yet exist. I see new possibilities. It takes others a while to see what I'm trying to describe.

Analyzer

I can take in large amounts of data and identify trends. When something goes wrong, I can sort through the facts and get to the bottom of it. I use a rational, logical approach to solving problems.

Planner

I anticipate what's needed. I can see where problems might arise and what we need to do to have everything work out well. I lay out what needs to be done and if people follow my plan, things go smoothly.

Coordinator

I like to orchestrate events. I bring people together and coordinate a host of details in order to pull off a project or event. I can keep track of a million details and bring it all together in the end.

Mentor

I enjoy developing people. I am often a coach or a sponsor for individuals or initiatives. I like to teach or advise individuals and I take an interest in them.

Promoter

I get others interested in new ideas, products or services. I generate enthusiasm by talking to lots of people and bring attention to new ideas, projects and possibilities.

Integrator

I bring people and ideas together. I see the interrelationships between ideas or tasks and connect them to achieve a common purpose.

Editor

I quickly see problems inherent in a new design or document or plan. I find the mistakes and flaws. If you don't like criticism, don't run your ideas by me. I like to improve an idea and make it better.

Developer

I like to develop new ideas, projects or businesses and make them successful. I can take a small project or idea and develop it into a large, successful project, prototype or business that has value and that others want.

Investigator

I like to research the facts. I gather data from many sources and synthesize what I find. I search out new information from diverse sources. I never have enough data. If it requires research, let me do it.

Broker

I like to put people in touch with one another. I have a broad network of friends and associates that I connect with each other. Others come to me to find valuable resources they need for projects.

Communicator

I like to communicate what's going on. I am often "in the know" about things. People come to me to find out what's happening.

Action Exercise

Discover your unique talent by answering these five questions and discussing them with friends who know you well:

1. What are your favorite projects or activities? At work? At home? In social situations?

2. What do you do even when no one is paying you to do it? At home? At work? When do you feel enthusiastic about an activity or event? What do you naturally want to do when no one is asking you to do anything?

3. What do others consistently ask you to do? What do your friends and coworkers want from you? When do they call you and for what?

4. When do you lose interest and enthusiasm for an activity or project because it does not use your talent?

5. When do others get annoyed with you because you're overusing your talent? When does your greatest strength become a liability?

Use the CARE instrument

Learn whether you're best at creating, refining an idea, executing projects, advancing new ideas or facilitating others by taking the CARE profile. You can order this instrument from my Web site at www.faithralston.com.

Give the CARE profile to members of your team and learn what each person contributes to the team. Discuss ways to optimize everyone's talent on the team. Have team members interview each other to identify their best talents. Explore ways to use each other's talents more fully on the team.

Also order my Play to Your Strength system to help clarify your leadership talents and attributes and what you contribute to others.

3. Do It

Once you've defined your talent, the next step is doing it. Begin contributing your talent in *any way* that you can. It requires *discipline* to stick with your talents. You make choices every day that move you closer to your talents or away from them.

Here are some ways to stay on track with your talent:

Seek work that uses your talent.

Rich, a computer programmer, has a strong talent for designing solutions. Yet he spends ninety percent of his time doing routine programming. To use his talent, he must seek out projects that require innovative solutions.

Go where you feel energized.

Hillary, the quality manager in a large corporation, feels out of place in her corporate function. She loves to work with customers and solve immediate problems. She misses being where the action is. Hillary needs to move closer to the field or find internal customers who want her action-oriented service.

Let go of what doesn't work.

Abdul is an engineer. He hates his new management job but stays in it to prove that he can do it. Every day he misses the "real work." Abdul needs to find a way to contribute as an engineer again. This may mean leaving management.

Embrace change to use your talents.

Kristi enjoys her job but dreams of going back to school and getting a degree. She hesitates and considers the impact on her life. After much thought she takes the plunge and goes back to school. Once there, she is extremely happy to be a student again.

Recognize that what you love to do will change.

Our talents evolve as we do. As our interests expand, new talents may rise to the surface. Our first thought is: What do I do with this interest? Or even: "This is an odd twist my life is taking." Rather than shy away from these soul-stirrings, it's important to let them lead us in new directions. A job may fit us like a glove for years and then suddenly it's not right anymore. It is uncomfortable and annoying when this happens, because it is much easier to stay where we are than it is to face the prospect of change!

Helping Others Use Our Talents

After naming our talents, we also need to tell others how to use us best. Don't assume they know! Tell others exactly what you can do *and* how it will benefit them. For example, if you are a good critical thinker, ask, "How might critical thinking be useful to my manager?" Then say to your manager, "I can help you anticipate problems. This will keep you from being blindsided by changes you didn't expect."

If you're a patient organizer, ask yourself, "How does being a patient organizer help my team?" Then say to team members, "I can organize this for you so that you can spend more time on the next phase of this project."

If you're an insightful advisor, ask yourself, "How does being an insightful advisor help my clients?" Then say to clients, "I have an idea that will save you time and money. Let's talk." The key to sharing your talent is to recognize how it benefits others. You must think from the other person's perspective and understand the benefit of your talent from their point of view.

Talents Pay Off

When we define our talents and shape work around them, we create opportunities that allow us to contribute more of who we are to the workplace. Take the example of Janice, a dietitian. She stopped working to raise two young children. When she returned to work she applied for jobs in the field of nutrition. After twenty-five interviews she had no job offer. Wisely Janice decided to make a course correction. She asked herself, "What do I love to do? What's important to me? What am I really good at?" She realized that she wanted to work as a consultant. She especially liked helping organizations to meet nutritional standards and comply with state regulations. She decided to call herself a "nutritional firefighter." Within weeks of changing direction and moving closer to her true interests, Janice received three consulting contracts. Defining her talent helped Janice discover which way to go.

Reshaping our contribution at work is a courageous and noble act. We need to talk openly about the process and how we are doing. The changes are not easy to make; plus, it is lonely to do it alone. I hope we will see the wisdom of supporting each other as we stretch, reach and strive to become more of who we are and find ways to offer our valuable gifts to the organizations we serve.

Business Reality #9: We contribute more when we love what we're doing.

Success Action: Leverage individual talents to deliver higher value.

Key Learnings

1. Talents are what we do easily and naturally.

2. When we're using our talents, we feel satisfied and fulfilled.

3. Focusing on talents is fundamentally different from focusing on our careers.

4. We usually don't recognize our talents as unique gifts.

5. It requires discipline to fully leverage our talents.

Chapter 10

Initiate Candid Conversations To Implement Change Faster

What's the point of having an opinion if you don't use it?

Peter Ralston, age 15

Successful change requires the ability to implement well. Management's track record as implementers is not stellar. Many strategies never get off the ground because leaders fail to address the emotional component.

- An electronics company sponsors customer-focused teams but fails to promote responsiveness to customer needs in daily transactions.
- A communication company trains its leaders to be more innovative but fails to successfully launch the new products.
- A computer manufacturer buys expensive new equipment but employees are reluctant to use it.

Words of commitment from management belie the reality as initiatives fade into oblivion. Managers are like promiscuous lovers who run from one romance to the next, enchanted at first and then greatly disappointed. Instead of looking at themselves to find the source of the problem, they search for a new love.

Despite management's best efforts, new strategies do not permeate the organization. Instead, organizations experience an implementation gap (see Figure 10-1).

Figure 10-1: Implementation gap

The following symptoms indicate that there is a gap between what leaders want and how employees are responding.

Top-level leaders:

- Do not agree on the changes needed.
- Harbor many doubts about the change.
- Fail to communicate why the change is needed.

Middle managers:

- Lack enthusiasm for the change.
- Do not make the change a priority.
- Fail to communicate the change to employees.

Employees:

- Feel left in the dark about what is happening.
- Are skeptical and mistrustful.
- Speculate about management's motives.

The most revealing symptom is when no one believes the change is actually going to happen.

Address Emotional Concerns

To become masters of change we must become experts at recognizing and addressing the issues. Regardless of how positive a change is, employees still have personal reactions and concerns about it. These concerns are predictable and felt by everyone when changes get underway. Emotional concerns center around these types of questions:

- Who will I report to?
- Will my work change? Is my job safe?
- Will I be a winner or a loser?
- Will I have a say in what happens?
- How am I going to get my regular work done and this, too?
- Do they really mean it? Can I trust them?

These understandable concerns can be useful. Managers need to make it safe for employees to express these concerns. If concerns aren't addressed, they can sabotage what managers are trying to accomplish. Silent concerns steal energy away from the work that needs to be done.

Candid Conversations

Managers can gain valuable insights and useful information by initiating candid conversations about emotional concerns. There are many benefits to engaging in candid conversations.

Candid conversations help us learn from our mistakes.

A high-tech firm purchases a production facility. Managers in the firm have no background in production. Very quickly the acquisition starts to divert profits away from the larger corporation. After three years of heavy investment and financial headaches, management sells the acquisition.

Later this management team has a courageous conversation about the acquisition disaster. In a facilitated working session, they review their decisions and learn from their mistakes. Specifically, they discuss:

- The events that took place.
- Key decisions made.
- The rationale behind their decisions.
- The personal needs and agendas involved.

At this meeting leaders agree on what went wrong and learn from the situation. No one in particular is blamed. They all accept responsibility for what happened. Candid conversations help this team learn from their mistakes and prevent them from happening in the future.

Candid conversations help us set boundaries.

In organizational life it's easier to say yes than to say no. Saying yes shows we're committed and willing to do what it takes to be successful. Saying no can brand us as uncooperative. But to achieve focus, sometimes even good ideas must be turned down. Candid conversations enable us to set limits and do a few things well.

Candid conversations help us commit to change.

By talking openly about the challenges we face, we can address them. Discussing the pros and cons of a change helps us integrate the change into our work life. If we avoid a difficult situation, it's harder to tackle the problems we encounter later. Knowing the problems helps us put the right solutions in place.

Candid conversations provide us with valuable insights as leaders.

The best leaders avidly seek feedback on themselves, their plans and current initiatives underway. Honest input from others can help guide our behavior and refine strategies toward favorable outcomes.

Facilitating Candid Conversations

Our honest thoughts and opinions are usually buried far beneath the surface. To access this potentially valuable resource, we must take the time to raise the issues or they will stay underground. Facilitating candid conversations is like drilling for oil. Oil is valuable but it's usually found underground. Once in a while a geyser erupts and oil spews all over the place. Most of the time we have to dig for the oil. It's the same with our opinions and concerns. Often they lie dormant. Occasionally, our feelings boil over and explode, but this is not productive.

When oil first comes to the surface, it's called crude oil. Crude oil must be refined before it's useful. When we first start talking candidly about real issues, the comments we make may be "crude" because we are frustrated and scared. Through the process of questioning, listening and dialogue, we can refine crude reactions and emotions into useful ideas to make things work better.

Five Steps for Candid Conversations

The following steps enable us to benefit from candid conversations and facilitate them with greater ease.

1. *Make it safe to talk about the real issues.*

To help people feel safe, say and mean the following:

- There will be no repercussions.
- It is safe to tell me what you think and feel.

- We reward candor here.
- There's no such thing as a stupid question.
- Thank you for speaking up.

2 Ask questions to raise the relevant issues.

Use these questions to learn people's reactions and opinions:

- What are your reactions to this idea?
- What are your honest opinions and genuine feelings about this idea?
- What reactions are you hesitant to share?
- If you didn't like this idea, what would you say?

3. Accept what you hear.

When people share their concerns, you must accept what you hear! This is the hardest part because employees may be unhappy, dislike the change or have misconceptions about what's really happening. If you try to change employees' views at this point, they will not be forthright and you won't learn what they are thinking. Allow the reactions, feelings and opinions to surface. During this step use these phrases:

- You are frustrated by...
- What makes you uncomfortable is...
- You're uncertain about...
- What you want to know more about is...
- What you're saying is...

Once the issues have surfaced, summarize what's been said and move on to the next step.

4. *Focus on what's needed and how to achieve it.*

In this step you want to move employees away from the problem and toward positive solutions. Remember that you are probably ready to move on long before they are. Shift the focus by asking employees to agree on what they want to achieve. Explore ways to achieve these goals. Come to an agreement on the desired outcome by asking:

- What do we agree we want in this situation?
- What will make this situation better?
- What do you really believe is possible?

Brainstorm for solutions by asking these questions:

- What suggestions do you have?
- How might we achieve our goals?
- What are the key things we could do?

5. *Specifically define the necessary next steps.*

Define the necessary next steps by asking:
- What actions can we take?
- What can we do to make this happen?
- What do you need from me to move forward?

Encouraging Candor

The following statements will promote candor in your discussions and regular meetings:

To hear unpopular views, use these comments:

- I'm glad you disagree with me.
- I want to hear your opinions.
- Who has a different point of view?
- Come to me with problems. I want to hear about them.

- What's the worst possibility that could happen if we try this idea?
- What haven't we anticipated?

To shed light on a situation, ask:

- What *don't* we know?
- What are some outrageous options?
- What have we ruled out?
- What haven't we discussed?
- What do we wish were true?

To identify feelings, ask:

- How are you feeling about this?
- How might others feel?
- Who could get hurt?
- Are you feeling...?
- What reactions do you have?

To surface frustrations, say:

- What we do that doesn't make sense is...
- I question the effectiveness of...
- If we were brave we would stop doing...
- I want to understand why we do...
- We can improve by doing...

To identify what's going right, say:

- Where are we doing this right?
- What successes do we have in this area?
- What can we learn from our successes?

Helpful Tips

Here are additional ways that you can foster candid conversations:

- Allow employees to raise their concerns without feeling that you have to alleviate their concerns. Realize that you can't always solve the problem. Simply sharing concerns is helpful.
- Be as honest as possible when you respond to employee concerns. You may need to say, "There may be layoffs because of this change" or "I don't know the answer to that yet."
- Reassure employees that you will keep them up to date on the changes taking place. Then do so.
- Invite questions, suggestions and input concerning the change.
- Involve employees in developing solutions to the issues that arise.

Getting started with candid conversations is the hardest part. There's a rhythm to these conversations. Comments are usually slow in coming at the beginning. Good questions are the key to getting off to a good start. When the comments come, participants are testing the water to see whether it's safe to share ideas. Gradually there are more and more responses and reactions. Questions are less important now and listening becomes the key. Simply listen closely and respond by restating their comments or saying, "Yes, and what else?" After a time, the intensity begins to wane and there's a lull in the conversation. Everyone relaxes. At this point you can turn the conversation toward the desired outcomes. Ask participants to clarify their desired outcomes and brainstorm about ways to achieve these. Then suddenly the conversation is over and you feel warm inside. You know that you and your employees are traveling together on the road to success.

Business Reality #10: Bottled-up concerns drain vital energy away from key initiatives.

Success Action: Initiate candid conversations to implement change faster.

Key Learnings

1. We will become better implementers by engaging in candid conversations about real concerns.
2. All change generates personal concerns.
3. Candid conversations help us learn from our past mistakes.
4. Candid conversations help us set boundaries.
5. Candid conversations help us commit to change.

Conclusion:

Call to Action

To eliminate corporate craziness and create productive and satisfying work environments, employees at every level must accept greater personal responsibility. In the past the unwritten contract between employees and their organizations encouraged employees to acquiesce and turn over responsibility for their professional and career satisfaction to others.

The implicit contract between organizations and employees went something like this: "The corporation will provide you with a job for life; in return you will pledge absolute loyalty and suppress much of what you think and feel." The expectation was that:

- The organization will provide you with a secure job.
- You are expected to contribute to the organization.
- If you disagree with the people in charge, it is best not to say so.

Remnants of these expectations continue to influence our attitudes today and prevent us from taking full responsibility for our work lives. Accepting personal responsibility is a radical departure from the past. It means we need to confront problems rather than allow them to fester. We must stop expecting management to fix everything that's wrong. The people above us don't have all the answers. We need to speak up about problems, recommend solutions, be willing to give and receive feedback and make changes in our attitudes and behaviors.

A top leader said to me: "I no longer believe that change starts at the top. If I wait for my management team to initiate the changes needed in this organization, it will take forever. I need individuals at every level who are willing to get involved and take initiative. I can't mandate change. I need everyone to believe in the vision and take action to bring about the changes needed. That's the only way it's ever going to happen."

Making Personal Choices

We must accept personal accountability for creating work environments where we can contribute our best. The choice is ours. No matter what's going on around us, we can choose to respond in a way that enhances the situation. As I am writing this conclusion a friend calls. In our phone conversations she is both excited and upset. She is excited because her husband finalized his decision to start a new business venture. After months of frustration and thwarted attempts to change his current job situation, he decided to leave his company and start a new business. It took enormous courage to make this decision because he enjoyed his staff and the security of working for a large corporation. I was delighted to hear her good news.

Next, our conversation turned to a different and grim topic. She told me that one of her colleagues at work recently committed suicide. She had just learned about his untimely death. The previous week this employee was terminated from his job. Rather than face an uncertain future, he chose to end his life. Everywhere in the organization employees gathered to talk and grieve the loss. I was deeply saddened by the news.

Later as I reflected on our conversation, I realized that we were talking about two individuals who made radically different choices. One chose to leave an unhealthy work situation and try his hand at a new venture; the other chose to end his life rather than face an uncertain future. These profoundly different choices put me in touch with the choices that confront us each day.

Accepting Personal Responsibility

To a far lesser extreme, we make life-giving or life-negating choices at work. Life-giving choices expand our vitality and enthusiasm for work; whereas life-negating choices deplete our energy and contribution. Everyday we make these fundamental choices. If we are unhappy, we have a choice about whether to face the situation or not. We may need to talk with a coworker, challenge a boss, speak up in a meeting, object to a decision or change our situation. The choice about whether to address the situation is ours alone to make.

Routinely, we need to ask ourselves these questions:

- Am I addressing the problems I see or passively going along with the situation?
- Am I speaking up about what I think needs to be done or tuning out and giving up?
- Am I finding my place of greatest contribution or biding my time and putting up with energy-draining work?

The answer to these questions determines whether we feel optimistic and hopeful about our work or feel de-energized and bored. More than ever it is our responsibility to address the challenges we face.

To do so we must become vulnerable and receptive to our emotions. Our emotions tell us when something is not right. As we learn to listen to our feelings and manage them effectively, we will know how to ask for what we need and work more effectively with others. If we or others are dissatisfied, we need to look our frustrations in the face and ask: "What can I do to change this situation? How can I help to create a work environment where we safely share our thoughts and feelings with each other, build high-trust relationships and generate enthusiasm about our future."

Acknowledging emotions helps us move toward our goals. As we learn to work with the power of emotions, we discover an incredible source of energy that can fuel our professional and work goals. Harnessing emotional energy enables us to achieve extraordinary personal and business results.

A Few of My Favorite Resources

Great Books

To communicate a compelling message...

Be Heard Now! Tap Into your Inner Speaker and Communicate With Ease, by Lee Glickstein. This book and set of audiotapes helps leaders learn to speak authentically. It describes how to set up and use Speaking Circles, a peer learning process that helps you touch others deeply by speaking from your deepest self.

To improve skills in conflict situations...

Tongue Fu! How to Deflect, Disarm, and Defuse Any Verbal Conflict, by Sam Horn. This practical book offers gems of wisdom on how to deal effectively with other people. Sam's actionable ideas and examples can fast-forward you past frustration and alienation into dialogue and positive interactions with others.

To become a great leader of people...

First, Break All the Rules, What the World's Greatest Managers Do Differently, by Marcus Buckingham and Curt Coffman. This material is based on solid research of over 80,000 managers in 400 companies by the Gallop organization. Leaders learn behaviors that will foster a committed and engaged workforce and the value of focusing on strengths instead of weaknesses to promote performance. I recommend this book for leaders who want to grasp their role as a leader.

To accept greater accountability for your life...

Life Strategies, Doing What Works, Doing What Matters, by Phillip C. McGraw, Ph.D. This book by Phillip McGraw, consultant to Oprah Winfrey, gives hard-hitting advice to help anyone take control of their life. If you or your employees are just "going through the motions" with no passion, goals or plan, McGraw wakes you up and holds you accountable for moving your life in the direction you want it to go. I recommend this book for leaders and employees who feel stuck in their work or life situations.

To ensure productive dialogue about difficult issues...

Difficult Conversations, How to Discuss What Matters Most, by Douglas Stone, Bruce Patton and Sheila Heen. How do you navigate a workplace fraught with office politics and tension? This book helps you stop swallowing your views and feeling like a doormat and start saying what you're thinking without a fight. This book is based on fifteen years of work at the Harvard Negotiation Projects. Use the ideas in this book to handle tough conversations more effectively.

To develop group facilitation skills...

Managers as Facilitators, A Practical Guide to Getting Work Done in a Changing Workplace, by Richard G. Weaver and John D. Farrell. This book helps managers become great facilitators. It's absolutely full of practical models and tools for managing groups, resolving conflicts and developing listening skills. Offers step-by-step guidance for real work situations.

To promote cross-functional communication...

The GE Way Field Book, by Robert Slater. If you're dealing with cross-functional barriers, this book helps you build a boundaryless organization. It offers practical ideas for changing your culture, focusing on results and working in a matrix organization. Especially valuable is the Work-Out process that engages multiple levels in generating business solutions. It includes self-assessment exercises, action steps, actual GE practices, and strategies and training materials.

To build trust and recover from betrayal...

Trust and Betrayal in the Workplace, Building Effective Relationships in Your Organization, by Dennis S. Reina and Michelle L. Reina. I use the content in this book to help leaders, employees and their organizations acknowledge betrayal, solidly recover from it and rebuild trust. Their recommendations are based on powerful new research. This is the first book to define trust and how to achieve it in workplace relationships.

To tackle implementation issues...

Close the Knowing Doing Gap, by Jeffrey Pfeffer and Robert Sutton. This book shows leaders how the dynamics of irrational fear, misguided measurement and internal competition thwart a company's success. This book explores the real issues that keep people and enterprises from taking right actions to fix problems in their organization. Read it to address barriers to organizational change.

To successfully implement change...

Journal to the Emerald City: Achieve a Competitive Edge by Achieving a Culture of Accountability, by Roger Conners, Tom Smith and Thomas Smith. The authors provide a concise model for creating and sustaining a culture of accountability at all levels of the organization. This book provides clear guidelines to help everyone in the organization focus on what they can do, instead of what they can't do, to contribute to the organization's success.

Useful Websites

To learn what current leaders are thinking and feeling...

http://www.thoughtleadergathering.com

The vision of the organization is nothing less than to change the DNA of leadership. Craig and Patricia Neal of Heartland Institute sponsor "Thought Leader Gatherings" to encourage dialogue among organizational leaders who are leading organizational change. If you live in San Francisco, Minneapolis or Boston, you can participate in these lively discussions. Check out their Website to gain insights and reflection from leaders who are transforming themselves and their organizations.

To enliven discussions about business challenges...

http://www.mgeneral.com

Tom Brown from Management General offers a delightful series of rewritten fairy tales to help business leaders engage in conversations about difficult issues such as budgeting, teamwork and change management. Use these tales to enliven team discussions and help you gain insights about business challenges. I like how these thought-provoking tales surface issues in a lighthearted way.

To build teamwork and facilitate change...

http://www.squarewheels.com

This site is jam-packed with tools and information on teamwork, creativity, change management and leadership development. You will discover more than five hundred pages of workshop ideas, training tools, exercises, jokes, team-building activities and creativity tools that are useful if you are a facilitator, consultant or manager interested in experiential learning.

To promote leadership development through peer coaching...

http://www.authenticityconsulting.com

Carter McNamara offers a vast amount of useful ideas to help you set up and run Leader Circles, a peer-based approach to leadership development and organizational change. Carter shares extensive research and offers practical tools for establishing and running action-learning groups. I recommend this site to anyone who wants to set up successful peer learning groups.

Recommended Films

You can order the following films from ChartHouse International Learning Corporation (1-800-328-3789).

To encourage employee accountability...

"Personal Accountability" video. This is one of the best films available on personal responsibility and accountability. John Miller's film is useful when you want to encourage employees to take responsibility for changes they can personally make to improve a situation.

To create a positive, committed work climate...

"Fish" and "Fish Stick" videos. These two films are excellent motivational films. In these films you learn how employees at

Seattle's famous Pike Place Fish Market create a culture focused on serving their customers. Any organization or department will benefit from these stimulating ways on how to create a climate that encourages both commitment and fun.

To strengthen communications between men and women at work...

"Talking 9 to 5" video. In this film, Debra Tannen, world renowned linguist, shares her insights on the differences in women's and men's communication styles and the impact these differences have on work effectiveness. Understand these concepts to ensure that good ideas are heard.

Leadership Style Instruments

You can order these instruments from my Website: http://www.faithralston.com

To help team members leverage their best talents...

Care Profile. This instrument helps teams benefit from the diverse talents of individuals on a team. I use the Care Profile to help team members identify their best contribution and discover ways to bring their best talents to the organization.

To strengthen communication among team members...

DiSC Profile. The DiSC Dimensions of Behavior profile helps team members learn about the strengths and weaknesses of their communication style and how to adapt their preferred style to others with a different style. I use the DiSC instrument to build teamwork and ease frustrations and conflict on a team. This instrument is available in a long version for coaching and team-building or an abbreviated version for training classes.

To improve individual listening skills...

Listening Skills Profile. The Personal Listening Profile® helps leaders identify their dominant listening style and select from five different types of listening skills to be more effective and purposeful listeners in a variety of situations.

Index

About the Author

Faith Ralston, Ph.D is an internationally recognized expert in organizational dynamics and business relationships.

Her company *LEAPS OF FAITH* works with 'Movers and Shakers' to achieve breakthrough performance. She helps top leadership teams *believe and achieve their vision by leveraging their best talents.*

Faith is an action-oriented business consultant, dynamic speaker and author. Her clients are among "The Best 100 Companies to Work For" and include American Express, Medtronic, General Mills, Price Warehouse and BlueCross BlueShield Minnesota. Faith's ideas and advice for business leaders are featured in *Industry Week*, Minnesota Public Radio, *Redbook*, Linkage Conferences, The Conference Board and syndicated newspapers around the counrty. Her best selling business book *Hidden Dynamics* has been published worldwide. Faith lives in Minneapolis, Minnesota with her family.

Contact Faith Ralston at:
LEAPS OF FAITH
311 Seymour Place
Minneapolis, MN 55414-4922 USA
Email: faith@faithralson.com
Website: faithralston.com

Printed in the United States
690900005BE

9 780759 674233